D0859733

TRUSTING
—— *the* ——
PEOPLE

"It is a paradoxical truth that tax rates are too high today and tax revenues are too low; and the soundest way to raise the revenues in the long run is to cut the rates now."

—John F. Kennedy, 1962

"By lowering everyone's tax rates all the way up the income scale, each of us will have a greater incentive to climb higher, to excel, to help America grow."

—Ronald Reagan, 1985

"The principle involved here is time-honored and true, and that is, it's your money. You shouldn't have to apologize for wanting to keep what you earn. To the contrary, the government should apologize for taking too much of it."

—Bob Dole, 1996

TRUSTING
— the —
PEOPLE

The Dole-Kemp Plan to Free the Economy and Create a Better America

*Balance the Budget
*Cut Taxes 15%
Raise Wages

Bob Dole and Jack Kemp

HarperCollins*Publishers*

HJ
2051
.D63
1996

TRUSTING THE PEOPLE Copyright © 1996 by Bob Dole
and Jack Kemp. All rights reserved. Printed in the United States
of America. No part of this book may be used or reproduced
in any manner whatsoever without written permission except
in the case of brief quotations embodied in critical articles
and reviews. For information address HarperCollins*Publishers*,
10 East 53rd Street, New York, N.Y. 10022-5299.

HarperCollins books may be purchased for educational,
business, or sales promotional use. For information, please
write: Special Markets Department, HarperCollins*Publishers*,
10 East 53rd Street, New York, N.Y. 10022-5299.

First Edition

Designed by Michele Bonomo

Library of Congress Cataloging-in-Publication Data is
available from the publisher.

96 97 98 99 00 ❖/HC 10 9 8 7 6 5 4 3 2 1

LONGWOOD COLLEGE LIBRARY
FARMVILLE, VIRGINIA 23901

CONTENTS

INTRODUCTION

Come November 5th, the American people will face a choice of two dramatically different paths into the 21st century.

As the Republican candidates for president and vice president, we believe in trusting the people to make more of their own decisions and keep more of their own earnings. Ours is a vision of growth, opportunity, and strong families through lower taxes; a vision of smaller government and greater responsibility entrusted to the individuals, families, and communities across this nation.

President Clinton would continue with *status quo* policies, even though his tax increases have mired America in sluggish growth, and left middle-class family incomes completely stagnant.

President Clinton, of course, aggressively defends his record, boasting that his Administration has given America the best economy in three decades.

But which economy is he talking about? If times are so good, why do Americans feel so anxious about their future? Why do *both* parents often have to work to make ends meet, when it used to take only one? Why is this the first recovery on record in which working Americans are being left behind? Why do so many of our fellow citizens feel like they are running on a treadmill and the treadmill is winning? And why do the majority of Americans believe our country is headed down the wrong track?

People are right to be concerned. Economic growth during the Clinton Administration has averaged a paltry 2.4 percent, which makes it the weakest of any expansion in the last century. Americans are working longer and harder, but taking home less.

Clearly, America is performing far below its potential. In fact, if our economy were a baseball team, we'd barely be batting .200. If we were a football team, we'd be scoring less than 10 points a game. And if we were Olympic athletes, we'd be lucky to collect a bronze.

Americans have never been content with mediocrity, and now is no time to start. America must do better and grow faster. We must get wages and living standards rising again for *all* our people. And that is exactly what the Dole-Kemp Economic Growth Plan is designed to do.

We are competing today in a global economy with tremendous opportunities. Many economies are growing at least three times faster than our own.

Unless we move decisively to close America's growth gap, we will fall behind in the race to create the new jobs and markets for the future.

That is why the challenge of invigorating growth will be the defining issue of the 1996 Presidential election. All Americans ought to be able to reach for their dreams and develop their God-given talents to the fullest—from college graduates looking for their first jobs, to young couples trying to build a nest egg, to families in our inner cities seeking a better life, to senior citizens nearing retirement and needing security.

In the face of such a challenge, however, President Clinton does not see America striding into the future with boldness, but tiptoeing with cautious baby steps. He and his economic team believe America should continue to grow slowly, for they fear faster growth will rekindle inflation.

History teaches otherwise. After Ronald Reagan's dramatic tax cut, America enjoyed a peacetime record—*92 straight months of growth* averaging almost 4 percent a year—nearly twice as strong as under Bill Clinton. Yet that robust era coincided with declining inflation and lower interest rates.

Bill Clinton, who ran on a pledge to lower taxes and then engineered the largest tax increase in our history, seems philosophically opposed to tax cuts. He likens tax relief to giving candy to children. He says he is "unalterably opposed" to our plan to provide tax relief to every working American. He says government "can't afford" to let people keep more of what they earn.

But isn't he forgetting something? It isn't the government's money. It's *your* money.

President Clinton refuses to acknowledge the plain moral truth that what government spends is created by the hard work of our people. Those earnings belong to the people, and they are not the government's to give away.

That is the dividing line in this election: Between an incumbent who raised taxes because he believes the American people don't send enough of their earnings to Washington; and challengers who will provide tax relief because they believe the American people send too much money to Washington.

We are eager to take our cause to the American people, for we know the magic of America does not lie in government, but in the dreams and courage of each human heart.

We are ready to marshal the power of a winning idea to get our country moving again and make America the jobs and growth capital of the world.

For starters, the Dole-Kemp plan stands on the twin pillars of a balanced budget and lower taxes. Those two goals are complementary, not contradictory, for we can only balance the budget on the shoulders of a strong growing economy. We cannot build a stronger economy without first cutting taxes, and then completely overhauling the tax code to make the tax system in America fairer, flatter, and simpler. And we cannot create more opportunity in America without reforming our schools, bringing common sense to our legal system, and rolling back burdensome regulations.

As President Kennedy observed in 1962, "Our true choice is not between tax reduction, on the one hand, and the avoidance of large federal deficits on the other . . .

"It is increasingly clear that an economy hampered by restrictive tax rates will never produce enough revenue to balance the budget—just as it will never produce enough jobs or profits."

True in President Kennedy's time, and equally true today, when taxes have become punitive and anti-growth.

So, when Bill Clinton says government can't "afford" to

lower taxes and balance the budget, we declare that we can't afford *not* to.

With a Republican Congress, we will scale back the size of a federal bureaucracy that has grown bigger than we can bear, more expensive than we can afford, and more powerful than a free people can endure.

And we will also move in dramatic fashion to lower tax rates and knock down the barriers to the American Dream and higher growth.

Let us count the ways:

First, we will cut tax rates for everybody—15 percent across the board.

Our tax cut is simple, fair, and treats everyone equally.

Second, we will provide families a $500 per child tax credit—permitting working families to subtract $500 for each child from its total tax bill, and putting that money back in their pockets, rather than sending it to Uncle Sam.

Third, we will cut the capital gains tax rate in half. Lowering the capital gains will enable the United States to flex its muscle in a world where most of our major competitors hardly tax capital gains at all. It will provide urgently needed fuel to the real engines of job creation—small businesses and aspiring entrepreneurs.

Fourth, a Dole-Kemp Administration will expand access to Individual Retirement Accounts for millions of Americans and *repeal* the 1993 Clinton tax increase on Social Security benefits.

Fifth, we will establish Opportunity Scholarships to help give millions of low- and middle-income families the financial ability to choose the best schools for their children.

And to further protect the American people against higher taxes, a Dole-Kemp Administration will demand a super-majority—a 60 percent vote of Congress—before income tax rates can ever again be raised on the American people.

Taken together, these reforms will cut taxes by as much as 70 percent for a married couple with two children earning $30,000 a year; by nearly 40 percent for a married couple with two children earning $50,000 a year; and by nearly

25 percent for a married couple with two children earning $100,000 a year.

As people do better, America will do better. As these incentives spark new ventures, new businesses, and more jobs, the lower tax rates, education reform, and a transformation of our regulatory and legal systems will quicken America's economic pulse. This will reawaken a sense of hope, vitality, and renewal in our cities, and lift our economy to a higher, more powerful level of performance.

Like all great choices, this election presents America with a question bigger than any two candidates. It's a question about ourselves. Have we become a "Grow Slow" society, content to let government spend our earnings for us, make our decisions for us, and let our wages stagnate and dreams fall away?

Or are we still the freest, most dynamic, productive, and hopeful people on Earth? Are we still in our hearts the country of Lincoln, who believed that opportunity was the birthright of every citizen in a country of boundless potential?

By denying America the chance to do better and grow faster, Bill Clinton and Al Gore have not only put themselves in a position of defending the status quo, but of asking millions of Americans to put their dreams on hold.

It is time for America to reach for greatness again. We can do it. We've done it many times before. All we must do is restore to government that trust in the people which has always been the source of our greatness.

Bob Dole
August 1996

Jack Kemp
August 1996

CHAPTER 1

A VISION OF FREEDOM:
Highlights of the Dole-Kemp Economic Growth Plan

The people of America are caught in a vise of high taxes and stagnant wages. Bill Clinton promised a middle-class tax cut. He broke that promise in a big way: He gave Americans the largest tax increase in history. Today, according to a study by the nonpartisan Tax Foundation, a typical American family pays nearly 40 percent of its earnings to government. We work from January 1 to May 7 every year *just to pay our tax bill.*

Common sense tells us that high tax rates punish, rather than reward, the efforts of the people. What is the incentive to strive harder, to save and invest and build, if at the end of the day the tax man takes nearly 40 percent of our earnings? High taxes today are stifling the American economy.

The Clinton Administration tells us to be content with an annual growth rate of 2.4 percent. They believe it's "the best we can do." We disagree. We believe the "grow slow" philosophy of the Clinton Administration represents a profoundly depressing view of America and our people. The American people can do better—as we have done many times before—if only we are given the chance.

Under the Clinton Administration—and just four years after

Bill Clinton's broken promise of a "middle-class tax cut"—
the total tax burden is the highest in U.S. history. Under Bill
Clinton, median-family income has gone up exactly zero.
Meanwhile:

- Economic growth has been slower under Bill Clinton
  than the year he was elected;
- Slower than the entire decade of the 1980s;
- Slower than the last five expansions;
- Slower than what we've averaged over our entire
  post–World War II history.

And that's after just four years. What would four *more*
years of the same mean for the American economy? The
signs are not good. Unless we cut taxes and free ourselves
from the grip of high taxes and regulation, we're facing
steady economic decline and more years of stagnant wages.
Unless we get government's own spending under control,
we'll be facing a budget crisis worse than any we've seen in
recent years, a crisis not confined to Washington but felt in
every household in America.

SIX COMMONSENSE STEPS TO A VIBRANT ECONOMY

The Dole-Kemp growth agenda is based on common-
sense economics: Leave more money with the people who
earn it, and they will put it into the productive uses that
drive our economy forward; creating jobs, building new businesses, and bringing about prosperity and greater opportunity for all.

But beyond simple economics, our plan is based on a
belief in the ability of people to spend their own earnings and
make their own decisions. It is founded on a belief in the
possibilities of freedom—a conviction that our whole economy is driven not by government, but by the efforts, hopes,
and dreams of individual Americans.

Here are the six key points of the Dole-Kemp plan for economic growth:

1. Pass a Balanced Budget Amendment to the U.S. Constitution
Last year, the Balanced Budget Amendment failed by just one vote. The reason? President Clinton and his allies in Congress waged a furious campaign to defeat it. In a Dole Administration, the amendment will have the full support of the president. *It will pass.* When it does, it will be one of the most sweeping and fundamental reforms ever enacted in Washington. And it will ensure that the federal budget *stays* balanced after 2002 and throughout the next century. Washington will no longer be able to pass on its unpaid bills to our children and grandchildren.

2. Balance the Budget by the Year 2002
Balancing the budget is a matter of congressional responsibility and presidential will. After four years of hollow promises from the Clinton Administration, a Dole Administration will balance the federal budget. By leaving more money with the people through a tax cut, we will get our economy moving again; spur investment and economic growth; and boost the wages of millions of working Americans.

That will bring in more revenue and help us balance the budget, but only if government does *its* part: The spending free-for-all of the Clinton years must come to an end. A Dole Administration will restore respect in Washington for the value of every tax dollar. We will use the line-item veto in defense of the taxpayer, cutting wasteful programs that serve only a few special interests.

With that resolve we will protect programs like Medicare and Social Security. The Clinton Administration claims to be the champion of Americans who depend upon these vital programs for their health and income. At the same time, the administration has done nothing to avert the crisis these programs will face unless we put Washington's finances in order.

3. Cut Taxes Across the Board and Replace the Current Tax Code

- Cut personal income tax rates by 15 percent *across the board.*
- *Ease the tax burden on parents* by creating a $500 per child tax credit.
- Reduce *by half* the capital gains tax for individuals and small business owners to increase *investment, job creation, and wages; and virtually eliminate it on the sale of homes.*
- *Repeal Bill Clinton's 1993 tax hike* on Social Security recipients.
- Expand Individual Retirement Accounts and establish a spousal IRA.
- *Protect American taxpayers* by requiring a three-fifths vote in Congress—a 60 percent super-majority—to raise income tax rates.
- Scrap the current tax code and replace it with a system that is *simpler, flatter,* and *fairer* to every taxpayer in America.

4. End the IRS As We Know It

- *Eliminate IRS filing for 40 million low- and middle-income taxpayers.*
- Put the *Service* back in "Internal Revenue Service" by requiring IRS employees to *help* taxpayers understand the law, rather than just punishing Americans for misapplying it.
- *Establish a one-year tax amnesty period* as a transition to a new and fairer tax system.
- *End abuses by overzealous IRS employees* by shifting the burden of proof in IRS audits from individuals to the government.
- *End abusive "life-style audits"* except where there is clear evidence of wrongdoing.

5. Reform Education and Job Training

- Help parents regain control of our schools by offering *Opportunity Scholarships for Children.*
- Allow low- and middle-income parents to *deduct all interest on student loans.*
- Allow parents to *set up tax-free Education Investment Accounts,* with contributions of up to $500 per child every year.
- Stop taxing workers who receive job search and placement assistance from their employers.
- Transform the federal government's 80-plus job-training programs into a single grant to the states, and encourage the states to experiment with vouchers and other innovative approaches to job training.

6. Cut Government Regulation and Reform Our Civil Courts

- *Bring fairness and common sense to federal regulation* by requiring a rigorous cost-benefit analysis for all new federal regulations.
- Establish a regulatory sun-setting task force to *weed out the needless and costly regulations* that hurt our economy.
- Demand a review of all federal regulations every 4 years to *eliminate harmful and outdated rules and mandates.*
- Enforce Paperwork Reduction Act to *free Americans from costly and time-consuming paperwork.*
- Reform joint and several liability to protect innocent people from abuses of our courts by trial lawyers.
- Limit punitive damage awards to *curtail the excesses of trial lawyers.*
- Promote early settlement of claims.
- *End abuse of our civil courts* by reforming contingency fee representation.
- Enact "auto choice" reforms to *cut insurance costs.*

CHAPTER 2

THE IMPACT OF THE DOLE-KEMP TAX CUTS

Where will the benefits of an across-the-board tax cut be felt the most? In every home and workplace in America. Taxpayers will keep more of the money they have earned. More money to spend and invest in their own families and their own futures. More money to save for retirement or a child's education. For businesses large and small, more money to invest in new ideas, new ventures, new equipment, and above all, in new jobs.

Government, after all, can spend wealth. It can redistribute wealth. But there's one thing it can't do: *It cannot create wealth.* Only the people themselves can do that. And you don't need a team of economic experts to prove the effects of a tax cut: The more money we leave with the taxpayers, the more they will do to drive our economy forward—the more free and vibrant and productive our whole economy will be.

That's just common sense. And just as clear is the reverse: The more money government takes from the people, the less they have to spend and build and invest—the less freedom they have to make decisions for themselves and their families.

PRESIDENT CLINTON'S BROKEN PROMISE

Bill Clinton promised a "middle-class tax cut" in 1992. But after he took office, he immediately broke that promise by imposing the single largest tax increase in the history of America—$260 billion. Nothing has done more to stifle our economy than that tax hike.

The Dole-Kemp tax cuts aim to spur economic growth, raise wages, create jobs, and let people keep more of what they earn. Our economy cannot grow and flourish under the burden of such high tax rates. But that alone isn't enough: *We need to balance the federal budget.*

CAN GOVERNMENT "AFFORD" TO CUT YOUR TAXES?

Few arguments ring more hollow that those of the Clinton Administration in its steadfast opposition to across-the-board tax cuts. Leaving the taxpayers of America with more of their own money, says the administration, will cost the government too much. Government can't "afford" to cut your taxes. Not only is this untrue; it reveals a classic big-government mindset.

Let's get something straight here: The wealth of America belongs to the people of America, not to their government. It's *your* money. And tax cuts are not a *cost* borne by government: *Taxes* are a cost borne by the people.

The big question in this campaign is not: Can government afford a tax cut? The issue is: Can the hard-working people of this country *afford* to pay nearly 40 percent of their income to government?

Our answer: A resounding *No.*

Today the costs of taxes on the people are too high—they are smothering investment and job creation, and causing a "grow slow" economy. A dramatic, across-the-board tax cut will get our economy moving again *and* help balance the budget, but only if government spending is brought under control.

At the heart of the Dole-Kemp plan are two fundamental ideas: Freedom and Responsibility. The people of America need more freedom to spend and invest their own earnings. And their government must be more responsible in spending the people's tax dollars. There is no contradiction in cutting taxes and balancing the budget. They go together as freedom and responsibility must always go together.

A BALANCED BUDGET AMENDMENT TO THE CONSTITUTION

Balancing the federal budget is essential, absolutely essential, to real and lasting economic growth. In 1995, the federal government paid over $230 billion in interest on the national debt. Today, nearly 40 cents of every dollar the federal government collects in personal income taxes goes to pay interest on the national debt.

The Dole-Kemp economic plan will balance the budget by the year 2002.

And if there was one great reform that should bring people of all parties together, surely this is it: A requirement in law that Congress not run up debts America cannot pay, debts we can only leave in shame to our children and grandchildren.

In the early days of a Dole-Kemp Administration, the Balanced Budget Amendment will come once again before Congress. This time it will pass. From there it will go before state legislatures in America with the full support of the President. It will swiftly become the law of the land. We are going to stop reckless deficit spending once and for all—for the good of this generation and all generations that follow.

A DEFICIT-FREE AMERICA: LOWER INTEREST RATES

The advantages for the present generation are dramatic enough. The effects of eliminating the federal deficit will be profound and immediate, felt in every household in America. Just consider interest rates. Today, interest rates are a heavy drag on our economy; they are the "stealth tax" everyone pays on top of our income tax bills. Our balanced budget plan will end that stealth tax. Interest rates will fall. According to the Congressional Joint Economic Committee, this alone will:

- *Save the typical family $36,000 on an average home mortgage.*
- *Save the typical family $1,400 on ordinary student loans.*
- *Reduce the cost of a typical car loan by $700.*

A 15 PERCENT TAX CUT FOR AMERICAN TAXPAYERS

The Dole-Kemp tax cut will reduce rates across the board in every tax bracket from top to bottom. Here's the exact breakdown on how a 15 percent tax cut will affect America's families. It is simple, fair, and will treat all Americans equally:

Federal Personal Income Tax Rates (%)		
Income Bracket	**Today**	**After 15% Cut**
$0–$40,100	15	12.8
$40,100–$96,900	28	23.8
$96,900–$147,700	31	26.4
$147,700–$263,750	36	30.6
$263,750 and up	39.6	33.7

Most American families are in those first two brackets. Based on a percentage of their income, they will be saving more than those taxpayers in the upper brackets.

• *Combined with the $500 per child tax credit, a family of four, earning $30,000 a year, will save nearly $1,300 in income taxes per year—a savings of 71 percent.*

Our critics say that's not much money. But for most Americans that's nothing to scoff at. For many, it's more than a two weeks' paycheck. It's a good share of a tuition bill. It's two months' rent, a mortgage payment, or an unexpected medical bill. But let the critics dismiss our tax cut. The Dole-Kemp plan is designed for people who still value $1,300.

A $500 TAX CREDIT FOR WORKING FAMILIES WITH CHILDREN

Under our present tax code, parents in working families have less and less time for the most important work of all—raising their children. The Tax Foundation estimates that a typical American family, in which both parents work, *pays more in total taxes than it spends on food, clothing, and housing combined.* Thirty-eight percent or more is spent in total taxes; 28 percent for food, clothing and housing.

Our plan will give families across America the tax relief they were promised in 1992, but never got. Under the Dole-Kemp Economic Growth Plan, low- and middle-income families will enjoy a $500 per child tax credit. That means that for every child under the age of 18, a family will see its tax bill cut by $500.

• *A family with four children will see its taxes reduced by at least $2,000.*

The amount of the credit will be reduced for married couples making more than $110,000 per year or $75,000 for single heads of households.

TAX FAIRNESS FOR AMERICA'S FAMILIES

One of the basic ideas of the Dole-Kemp plan for economic growth is that parents in America should not pay a dime to the government until they can first provide the essentials for their own family. Under current tax rates, many families are just barely getting by. Both parents often have to work just to make ends meet. Two wages are required where one income used to be enough. Here's the breakdown on the savings families can expect under a Dole-Kemp Administration:

- *A married couple with two children earning $30,000 will save $1,272 per year.*
- *A married couple with two children earning $50,000 will save $1,657 per year.*
- *A married couple with no children earning $50,000 will save $779 per year.*
- *A retired couple with no children earning $60,000 will save $1,727 per year.*
- *A single taxpayer with no children earning $30,000 will save $519 per year.*

A CAPITAL GAINS TAX CUT TO SPUR SAVINGS AND INVESTMENT

Over half of the people who pay taxes on capital gains earn less than $50,000 a year. A high capital gains tax rate punishes Americans who make wise investments, families who see the value of their homes increase, and entrepreneurs who create growing businesses. A good part of our economy is today frozen in place because people—quite sensibly—are holding onto assets to avoid being hit with a high capital gains tax. Billions of dollars are locked in those assets, billions that could be going into new investments that create jobs and stimulate our economy.

Cut the capital gains tax, and families that sell their businesses, homes, or farms will be able to keep a far greater portion of whatever profit they make. Perhaps most important, a cut in the capital gains tax rates will spur small and growing businesses—the very businesses that create the most new jobs in our country.

Specifically, our plan will:

- *Cut the capital gains tax rate in half, from 28 percent to 14 percent.*
- *Cut it still further for those taxpayers who are in the 15 percent tax bracket—down to a 7.5 percent capital gains tax rate.*

For example, under current law, if a family invested $10,000 in a stock in 1989 and sold it today for $25,000, they would be required to pay $4,200 on the profit they have made. Under the Dole-Kemp Economic Growth Plan, cutting the capital gains rate in half means that they could sell their stock and pay only $2,100 in capital gains taxes—a *savings of $2,100.*

A CAPITAL GAINS TAX CUT FOR HOMEOWNERS

For many American families, a first home is the biggest investment they ever make. Under current law, if you sell your house and use the proceeds to buy another house— within two years—you don't get taxed. But if you use the proceeds to invest in something else, or if you keep the money, you get taxed. Under our plan:

- *Homeowners will be allowed to exclude from taxation $250,000–$500,000 on a gain made from the sale of a home.*

The home would have to be the principal residence where the taxpayer resided for at least three of the preceding five years. For taxpayers who had lived in their homes for at least ten years, the $250,000 would be increased to up to $500,000.

EXPAND INDIVIDUAL RETIREMENT ACCOUNTS (IRAS) TO ENCOURAGE SAVINGS

Our plan also aims to reduce the disincentives for Americans to save. We will build on existing IRAs by creating *American Dream Savings Accounts*. These special savings accounts will work very much like IRAs except that they will allow participants to make after-tax contributions and earn interest tax-free. Under the Dole-Kemp plan, Americans could also make penalty-free withdrawals from an American Dream Account to help finance the purchase of a first home, pay for college expenses, or defray medical costs.

A NEW IRA FOR SPOUSES

Under current law, IRAs are a benefit for working individuals, but they discriminate against spouses who choose to stay at home, often to raise children. Our plan will put an end to this unfair treatment of married couples who decide that one spouse will stay at home. Under Dole-Kemp, a $2,000 contribution can be made into an IRA on behalf of a spouse working in the home.

PENALTY-FREE IRA WITHDRAWALS FOR HIGHER EDUCATION

Our present tax code is in many ways hostile to parents across America, especially those trying to save money for a child's college education. Under current law, for example, a withdrawal made from an Individual Retirement Account is subject to a 10 percent penalty tax—even if the money is going to pay for tuition. This is wrong. We should not discourage savings for education. Our plan will abolish that provision of the tax code, among many others that place burdens on the families of America. Specifically, under Dole-Kemp, individuals would be eligible to:

- *Withdraw funds from an IRA account to pay for tuition or related higher-education costs for themselves, a child, or a spouse without any penalty.*

EDUCATION INVESTMENT ACCOUNTS

To give parents added incentive to save for their child's college education, the Dole-Kemp plan will establish "Education Investment Accounts" for low- and middle-income parents. These accounts can be established for their children up to the age of 18. The $500 per child tax credit or other funds may be placed into these accounts, up to a limit of $500 per child, per year.

- *Contributions to the Education Investment Accounts, along with the interest accrued, will be tax-free if the funds are left in the account for at least five years.*
- *Under this provision, parents who placed $500 each year into their Education Investment Accounts would—at 7% interest rates—accrue $18,689 in tax-free dollars after 18 years.*

Money can be withdrawn from these accounts to pay for tuition, fees, books, computers, and other expenses at an accredited college, university, or other post-secondary institution of higher learning.

RESTORE THE INTEREST DEDUCTION FOR STUDENT LOANS

Most parents in America worry about the ever-rising cost of college tuition. Many can't afford it at all and have to take out student loans. But even when student loans are available, the student and his or her family know they face a long period of repaying those loans with interest.

Our tax system should be designed to make it easier for Americans to get access to higher education. There is no better way to expand opportunity. That is why the Dole-Kemp Economic Growth Plan restores a sensible deduction to the tax code that will benefit students and their families. Under this provision, low- and middle-income individuals who are paying off their student loans will be able to:

- *Deduct the interest paid on qualified student loans for five years.*

REPEAL THE CLINTON TAX HIKE ON SOCIAL SECURITY

One of the most devastating features of the Clinton Tax of 1993, the largest tax hike in our history, was the extra tax it imposed on elderly Americans living on fixed incomes. This was not merely a tax hike on the "wealthy" retirees; seniors with incomes as low as $34,000 saw their taxes on Social Security benefits go up. As a result of the Clinton tax increases, *85 percent of Social Security benefits became subject to federal taxation.*

This is wrong. The Dole-Kemp plan will reverse this punitive and arbitrary tax on seniors and restore Social Security taxes to their pre-1994 levels. The result will be that seniors who depend on Social Security income will be able to keep more of their money, rather than seeing the federal tax bill eat away at it.

TAX RELIEF FOR FAMILY-OWNED BUSINESSES

Small business owners around America put their heart and soul into their businesses. What does government do for them in return? Often our tax laws seem designed to punish their hard efforts. For example, current law applies a high estate tax rate to family businesses that makes it increasingly difficult to keep a business or farm in the family following the owner's death. The Dole-Kemp plan will:

- *Provide special estate tax treatment for qualified family-owned businesses by excluding an additional $1,000,000 of value from an estate.*

This critical reform will allow families to keep an inherited business or farm in the family, rather than having to sell it simply to pay the taxes levied by the federal government.

SIMPLIFYING THE TAX CODE FOR INDEPENDENT CONTRACTORS AND HOME-BASED BUSINESSES

Home-based businesses are among the fastest growing sectors of the American economy. Many of these businesses include Americans who choose to work as "independent contractors." But the Byzantine rules and regulations from the Internal Revenue Service vastly complicate the lives of these self-employed entrepreneurs. The reward for their drive and initiative seems to be distrust, mounting paperwork, and often harassment from the IRS.

It is just incredible that our tax laws are so hostile to such businesses: These are the folks who make our economy grow.

Among other reforms helpful to America's home-based entrepreneurs, the Dole-Kemp Economic Growth Plan will establish clear and simple requirements for individuals who want to be treated as independent contractors. It will also expunge from the tax code existing IRS rules that penalize home-based businesses if an individual spends some time at another business location outside of the home.

CHAPTER 3

TAX RELIEF FOR AMERICAN FAMILIES

We believe America's tax code should be simple, fair, uniform, and based on clear and enduring principles of law. Tax laws should not be arbitrary, changing every few years according to who's running Congress. Our tax code should not give special preference to one group of Americans over the other, rewarding those with the money and clout to hire lobbyists in Washington. Above all, taxes should not overly burden the great middle class on which this country's economic future will always depend.

Under the Clinton Administration, tax policy has failed on all counts. The tax code is more complex and incomprehensible than ever. Taxes are imposed arbitrarily—on workers, seniors, college students, small business owners, almost anyone in sight—with no regard to their effect on the lives and livelihoods of the people being taxed. And the great middle class, promised a "middle-class tax cut" in 1992, instead got hit by the biggest tax hike in our country's history.

TAX RELIEF FOR ALL TAXPAYERS

Our 15 percent tax cut is simple, fair, and will apply across the board. Other tax relief measures will be felt differently by different families and individuals depending on circumstance. The $500 per child tax credit helps families with young children. The deduction for student loan interest helps the parents of college-age children. Many retired seniors will gain from the rollback of the Social Security tax hike imposed by President Clinton. But the core of the plan applies across the board: Taxpayers will see their tax rates cut by 15 percent.

How will these changes affect you and your family? Americans have long been accustomed to the overly complicated tax rules that make it difficult to determine how much they will owe the federal government every April 15. The aim of the Dole-Kemp tax-cutting plan is to make the system simpler and to ensure that Americans pay less in federal income taxes.

How much will a typical family save? Just take a look at the table below:

YOUR INCOME UNDER THE DOLE-KEMP TAX CUT

Married couple, two children, earning $30,000 per year

Federal Income Tax Under Current Law:	$1,781
Federal Income Tax Under Dole Plan:	$508
Savings Under Dole Plan:	$1,272
Percentage Change in Federal Income Tax:	- 71.4%

Married couple, two children, earning $50,000 per year

Federal Income Tax Under Current Law:	$4,380
Federal Income Tax Under Dole Plan:	$2,723
Savings Under Dole Plan:	$1,657
Percentage Change in Federal Income Tax:	- 37.8%

Married couple, two children, earning $100,000 per year
Federal Income Tax Under Current Law: $13,858
Federal Income Tax Under Dole Plan: $10,583
Savings Under Dole Plan: $3,275
Percentage Change in Federal Income Tax: *- 23.6%*

Married couple, no children, earning $50,000 per year
Federal Income Tax Under Current Law: $5,190
Federal Income Tax Under Dole Plan: $4,412
Savings Under Dole Plan: $779
Percentage Change in Federal Income Tax: *- 15.0%*

Retired couple, no dependent children, earning $60,000 per year
Federal Income Tax Under Current Law: $6,802
Federal Income Tax Under Dole Plan: $5,075
Savings Under Dole Plan: $1,727
Percentage Change in Federal Income Tax: *- 25.4%*

Single taxpayer, no dependent children, earning $30,000 per year
Federal Income Tax Under Current Law: $3,458
Federal Income Tax Under Dole Plan: $2,939
Savings Under Dole Plan: $519
Percentage Change in Federal Income Tax: *- 15.0%*

TAX CUTS ACROSS THE COUNTRY

These tax cuts will benefit families in every state—and that's not counting the overall effects of lower taxes on our economy. The average family with children will end up saving $1,689 on its federal tax bill each year. Here are the effects state by state:

The Dole-Kemp Tax Cut:

A State-by-State Analysis of Annual Tax Savings[1]

State	Total Tax Savings	Savings per Family[2]
Alabama	$1,133,986,343	$1,745
Alaska	$214,090,809	$1,901
Arizona	$1,024,713,327	$1,755
Arkansas	$584,934,945	$1,508
California	$9,108,930,533	$1,684
Colorado	$1,358,280,081	$1,731
Connecticut	$1,349,759,488	$1,688
Delaware	$247,072,562	$1,654
District of Columbia	$236,714,552	$1,401
Florida	$3,877,644,228	$1,626
Georgia	$2,075,738,941	$1,685
Hawaii	$394,664,539	$1,671
Idaho	$217,102,820	$1,730
Illinois	$3,962,435,509	$1,752
Indiana	$1,884,582,082	$1,655
Iowa	$1,065,346,079	$1,784
Kansas	$824,036,896	$1,842
Kentucky	$1,102,333,990	$1,622
Louisiana	$1,088,848,907	$1,745
Maine	$372,485,025	$1,667
Maryland	$1,881,489,229	$1,672
Massachusetts	$2,072,920,985	$1,768
Michigan	$3,126,367,750	$1,796
Minnesota	$1,740,499,958	$1,826
Mississippi	$558,494,850	$1,496
Missouri	$1,617,290,971	$1,761
Montana	$152,966,158	$1,449
Nebraska	$479,303,153	$1,722
Nevada	$424,084,274	$1,660

New Hampshire	$379,428,321	$1,629
New Jersey	$2,858,338,322	$1,727
New Mexico	$429,900,590	$1,795
New York	$5,362,883,023	$1,646
North Carolina	$1,931,542,715	$1,555
North Dakota	$199,682,267	$1,754
Ohio	$3,561,562,739	$1,609
Oklahoma	$872,059,764	$1,615
Oregon	$1,003,133,203	$1,726
Pennsylvania	$3,729,241,197	$1,677
Rhode Island	$303,566,489	$1,684
South Carolina	$976,368,872	$1,497
South Dakota	$201,726,895	$1,626
Tennessee	$1,522,877,233	$1,584
Texas	$5,007,395,712	$1,692
Utah	$626,570,940	$2,009
Vermont	$220,015,557	$1,728
Virginia	$2,229,569,659	$1,639
Washington	$1,995,421,373	$1,737
West Virginia	$437,284,324	$1,673
Wisconsin	$1,752,128,411	$1,737
Wyoming	$159,367,440	$1,886
Other Regions	$338,518,258	$1,728
United States	$80,275,702,288	$1,689

Source: Office of Senator Spencer Abraham (R-MI), using the Heritage Foundation's Tax Simulation Model.

[1] Tax savings from fully phased-in 15 percent income tax cut and $500 per child tax credit only.

[2] Annual mean tax savings per family.

WHAT ECONOMIC GROWTH MEANS FOR AMERICANS

The comprehensive Dole-Kemp plan is designed to achieve an annual growth rate of 3.5 percent. Yes, that goal is ambitious. But we believe, with the right policies, America can meet this goal. What would it mean for America's families?

Like all great economic reforms, the effects would ripple out into our economy, helping, in time, every household. For example, a growth rate of 3.5 percent per year would *double* the real income of the average American citizen within a generation.

Consider the other effects, both short and long term:

- Median-family income is now about $40,000 per year. If America achieves our goal of a 3.5 percent annual growth rate, the median-family income for the next generation will be about $80,000 per year, and that's in real dollars adjusted for inflation.
- Per capita income would rise from $17,000 today to $34,000 for the next generation.

No longer would people worry that, for the first time in American history, the next generation will do worse than the previous one. Have a look at the chart on the following page. It shows what would happen to real earnings—wages, salaries, and benefits—if our goal is met, compared with what would happen if earnings continued to stagnate as they have under President Clinton.

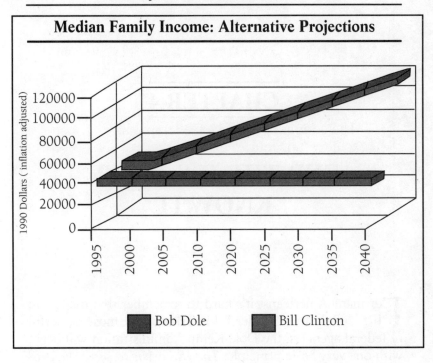

CHAPTER 4

END THE IRS AS WE KNOW IT

For many Americans, it's hard to remember that the "S" in IRS stands for "Service." In curbing that most powerful of federal agencies, the Dole-Kemp Administration will begin with one very basic principle: *The IRS exists to serve the people of this country, and not the other way around.*

The IRS performs the vital work of collecting revenue for the federal government—never a popular task. But that duty does not give the IRS a license to harass, intimidate, and abuse the trust of the people of America. The IRS has seriously abused that trust. It needs to be reined in. The IRS needs to be, not merely reformed, but *transformed.* The IRS, as we know it today, must be abolished. Under our plan, it will be.

AN END TO IRS HARASSMENT

A recent bill before Congress reflects the basic difference in outlook between the Clinton Administration and a Dole-Kemp Administration.

The bill was designed to cut the budget of the IRS by more than 10 percent—a step toward reining in the agency. It also would have put an end to some of the more abusive practices employed by the IRS against taxpayers. We favored those cuts because the IRS already has a staff five times as big as the FBI, and twice the size of the CIA. With more than 100,000 employees, and a budget that has doubled in just the past decade, the IRS is already too big.

But the Clinton Administration threatened a veto, calling any cuts to the IRS unacceptable. A White House spokesman fretted to reporters that such cuts in the IRS budget would "cripple our tax system."

We see it exactly the other way around: *Our tax system is crippling the American economy.*

THE IRS: AN AGENCY OUT OF CONTROL

We have some very different ideas about what is "unacceptable." When our representatives in Congress try to curtail the powers of the IRS, that isn't "unacceptable". That's democracy in action. The people have every right to control the IRS. And there's a growing feeling today that we'd better do it soon.

What is unacceptable to us is a tax code so complicated that tens of millions of Americans have to hire trained experts in tax law just to file their returns.

What's unacceptable is the cost in time, money, and grief inflicted by the IRS on millions of Americans trying their best to make a living and pay their taxes.

Also unacceptable are the arbitrary methods the IRS has taken to using against honest citizens, often with no evidence at all of tax evasion.

And even more unacceptable is the feeling of utter powerlessness the ordinary citizen feels when confronted with the often crass and callous methods of the IRS.

Every year, more than a million and a half Americans face liens, sometimes with no warning at all. IRS agents are actually rewarded on the basis of their "take" in confiscating property, which perhaps just may explain why penalties imposed by the IRS have risen tenfold since 1980.

The IRS today has powers unknown to the Justice Department or FBI. It requires no warrant to demand from banks or credit agencies just about any information it wants. Where are the civil libertarians on the left who usually rise in opposition to such unfettered power? As we see it, such methods are unacceptable in a free society. Under the Dole-Kemp plan, we are going to put a stop to it.

No "Life-style Audits" Without Cause

Each year, at random, the IRS subjects thousands of Americans to "life-style audits." There need be no hint of wrongdoing. The process is completely arbitrary. IRS Commissioner Margaret Miller, a Clinton appointee, declared in defense of these methods that henceforth the IRS "will audit the taxpayer, not just the tax return."

We have a simple reply to the commissioner and president who appointed her: *Unacceptable.*

In a free society, citizens enjoy the presumption of innocence until there is evidence of wrongdoing. They should not be randomly summoned before government agencies to account for their life, work, and income in the absence of any evidence of criminal conduct. It is wrong. It is an abuse of power. In a Dole-Kemp Administration, the entire practice will be put to a stop.

Here is our plan to reform the IRS:

- *Shift the burden of proof in IRS audits from the individual back to the federal government.*

No more "life-style audits" carried out with no evidence of wrongdoing. The government has no business investigating people without clear and reasonable grounds. Today, American taxpayers are presumed guilty until proven innocent. We're going to reverse that presumption and instruct the IRS to start treating people with the consideration, courtesy, and respect due to every honest, hard-working taxpayer in America.

- *Eliminate IRS filing for more than 40 million low- and middle-income taxpayers.*

There is no reason at all why a person with only wage income and some minimal investment income should even be required to file. Under the Dole-Kemp plan, low- and middle-income taxpayers with investment income of $250 or less would no longer be required to file a tax return. All of their taxes would be collected through withholding.

- *Establish a one-year amnesty as America moves to a new, simpler, and fairer tax system.*

During this transition, individuals would be permitted to pay back taxes without penalty or interest charges.

- *Shift IRS personnel and resources to the front-end of the tax filing process rather than the back-end.*

IRS employees should be dedicated to helping taxpayers file their returns correctly, not simply waiting until they make a mistake and then pouncing on them with an audit. The IRS should be on the side of the taxpayer—helping us to comply with the law, and not just punishing us when we're unable to make sense of an incomprehensible, unfair, and unjust tax system.

CHAPTER 5

REPLACE THE TAX CODE

The Dole-Kemp 15 percent, across-the-board tax cut for America's families is Step One. But tax reform won't end there in the Dole-Kemp Administration. If we are going to make the American economy great again, if we are going to give the people of this country lasting protection from tax tyranny, we need to work toward a flatter, fairer, simpler tax system.

The long-term goal of serious tax reform must be the overhaul of the federal tax code. In achieving that goal, we should bear in mind these basic principles:

FAIRNESS

- *Restore fairness to our tax laws by ending, once and for all, special interest loopholes, and by taxing income at lower tax rates.*

Tax laws should apply equally to all. No loopholes designed for a privileged few. No special favors for those with the money to buy the influence of tax lobbyists.

Instead of stating simple principles and clear definitions, applicable to all Americans, our tax code has become a gigantic

mass of exemptions, qualifiers, and rules to ensnare some
while letting others off the hook. Our reforms will put an
end to all that. It will once again be a code of laws the people
can both understand and respect.

Our plan aims to restore one basic principle: *Tax laws
should treat all Americans equally. Tax relief should be given
to all taxpayers.*

SIMPLICITY

- *Let most taxpayers file with a postcard-sized form
  or not be required to file a return at all.*

Why do we need a federal tax code running tens of thousands of pages? We don't. Why do we need some 480 different tax forms, and another 280 forms *explaining* those 480
forms? We don't. What any sane tax system needs is one
rule: *Keep it simple!*

In all its complexity, our tax code is today unfair in
almost every way imaginable: Our tax laws are beyond the
comprehension of most mortals. That's why tens of millions
of us need the help of an accountant to file our tax returns.
And often even the accountants cannot make sense of the tax
code. As most accountants will tell you, much of what they
do is just skilled guesswork.

- *Money magazine did a survey asking 50 different
  accountants to handle a single hypothetical tax
  return. The result? Fifty different returns with 50
  different tax bills.*

Across our economy, the total costs of complying with
the tax code are just staggering. One study added up all these
costs—in lost time, accounting, the budget of the IRS itself,
the paperwork inflicted on taxpayers. It arrived at an estimate of *5.4 billion man hours spent in complying with the
tax code.*

What a terrible waste of human energy! That's time that people across America could be working productively or spending with their families. It is also a tremendous drag on productivity. But that's the price we're paying today to meet the demands of a burdensome and irrational tax code.

PRO-GROWTH

- *End the bias against savings and investment in our tax laws.*

Under the current system, income that is used for consumption is taxed once, while income that is saved is taxed again and again. Business owners large and small must figure out elaborate depreciation schedules which often leave them paying taxes before they've even recovered the cost of their investment. Not only is that unfair to many taxpayers—it drives up the costs of doing business, discourages investment, and hurts our whole economy.

The Dole-Kemp tax reforms begin the process of reducing the high taxes on certain types of income, such as capital gains. In doing so, it seeks to stop punishing investment and savings.

FAIRNESS TO AMERICAN WORKERS

- *Relieve the tax burden on working Americans by allowing for the deductibility of the payroll tax.*

Working Americans pay taxes every time they receive a paycheck from their employers. Many employees actually pay more in payroll taxes than they do in federal income taxes. We want to move toward a system that permits them to deduct the payroll tax from their overall tax bill; so more money will be directed back to the working taxpayer.

PROTECTS SOCIAL SECURITY

- *Keep our pledge to elderly and retired Americans living on fixed incomes.*

Above all, this means a stable tax system that doesn't have to increase taxes on the Social Security benefits on which millions of Americans depend. But the same principle applies to us all. When tax laws are stable, people can make long-term decisions for themselves, their families, and their businesses without fear that overnight everything will change.

Stability is important to elderly Americans living on fixed incomes. How did the Clinton tax hike affect them? It raised the tax on their benefits even higher, so that 85 percent of the Social Security payments the government makes are now subject to taxes. This was just plain wrong, and our plan will reverse it. The Kemp-Dole plan will repeal that tax on elderly Americans.

PERMANENT SAFEGUARDS AGAINST TAX INCREASES

- *Require a 60 percent vote of Congress—a super-majority—to raise income tax rates.*

Our tax laws have seen *31 major changes in just 40 years.* Such constant changes in tax code rates, apart from their unfairness to working Americans, are extremely destabilizing to our whole economy. We need to put your earnings farther from the reach of government. Raising taxes should not be done according to political whim or the shifting balance of power in Washington. It's a serious matter, one of the most serious responsibilities government has. It's serious enough, we believe, to require the consent of 60 percent of the Congress and not a mere majority.

CHAPTER 6

CUTTING TAXES:
The Right Thing to Do

It is wrong for government to take from the taxpayer one penny more than is absolutely necessary for the essential functions of government.

When the government taxes too much, it isn't just hurting the economy. It isn't just taking the people's money. It is breaking a trust. It is taking away their freedom. Few things shake the confidence of the people in their government more than the abuse of the power to tax.

Those who think tax reform is just about money are missing the bigger point. The issue is freedom. It's the freedom of every wage earner in America trying to make his or her way in the world. It's the freedom to keep what we have earned by the sweat of our own labor.

That's what the Dole-Kemp tax cut is all about: Not just freeing up investment capital in our economy, but freeing the working people of this country to seek better lives for themselves and their children.

Is Cutting Your Taxes "Risky"?

Opponents of our tax cut plan talk as if letting people keep more of what they earn were some radical, irresponsible, "risky" new idea. That's a familiar mindset in Washington: It's always "risky," they say, to let the people keep their own money, but "responsible" to raise your taxes and expand government.

We don't see it that way. In a democracy, responsibility lies in keeping promises and trusting in the people. Was it "responsible" of Bill Clinton to promise you a middle-class tax cut, and then break that pledge? Was it "responsible" to saddle millions of working families and small businesses with an extra tax burden, when they're already paying almost 40 percent of their income to support government?

And what about that "risk" our critics talk about? As we see it, the real risk is in letting government take away more and more of the people's earnings. The risk is in letting Washington make more and more of our decisions for us. Our whole country, after all, is based on the proposition that individual men and women, left to make their own choices, will act more wisely than any government acting on their behalf.

A TRADITION OF TAX FAIRNESS

That's one reason for our long history of distrusting high taxation. It's often forgotten that for most of our life as a nation, America had no income tax at all. It took a constitutional amendment to enact the income tax in 1913.

Even after the income tax was imposed, it was imposed very carefully. Only the very wealthy had to pay. And the top rate was just 7 percent—less than half the *lowest* tax rate today.

As late as 1930 the average American worker was paying just 12 percent of his or her income to the government. By 1950 Americans were paying an average of 25 percent of their income to government at all levels. Today we're paying just under 40 percent of our income to support government.

In all, federal taxes today consume 20.5 percent of our nation's total output—the gross domestic product—according to the Department of Commerce. At the peak of World War II in 1945 the federal government only took 20.1 percent. The *total* government tax burden (federal, state, and local) is at the highest level ever—a staggering 31.4 percent of total national income.

TOTAL GOVERNMENT RECEIPTS HIT RECORD HIGH

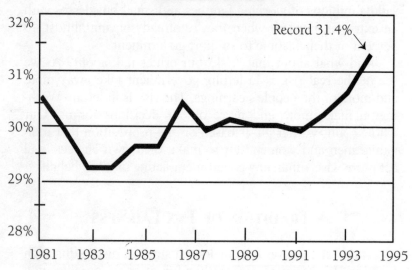

Sources: Department of Commerce; JEC.

THE GROWING MIDDLE-CLASS TAX BURDEN

How is the weight of the tax burden felt at the bottom? The lowest federal income tax rate today is 15 percent. Added to that is another 15 percent in payroll taxes. On top of that—another 10 percent or so in state and local taxes. Today, middle-class families are paying tax rates previously reserved for the rich. The chart on the next page shows what families across America know already—that their taxes have been steadily rising without relief:

1995 TAX BURDEN ON THE TYPICAL AMERICAN FAMILY[1]

Federal Income Tax	$4,926
Payroll Taxes:	
Employee Portion	$3,822
Employer Portion	$3,822
Other Federal Taxes	$2,244
Total Federal Taxes	**$14,814**
Total State/Local Taxes	**$6,506**
Total Taxes	**$21,320**
After Tax Income	$34,541

Total Taxes as a Percent of Income[2]
38.2%

[1] Two-earner family of four (median family income=$52,039), 1995 estimate.

[2] Effective tax rate calculation adds employer's share of the payroll tax to the family's income.

Sources: Tax Foundation; U.S. Bureau of the Census.

Is it fair to tax the working families in our country at nearly 40 percent? Is it right that today's high tax rates are forcing both parents in working families across America to take jobs, with one parent often working just to cover the family tax bill?

Our answer is an unequivocal *No.* We believe such high levels of taxation are wrong. They are indefensible. They violate our deepest principles and best instincts as a people. Government should be helping to *lift* the burdens on working families, not adding to them.

THE CLINTON RECORD: HIGHER TAXES, LOWERED EXPECTATIONS

President Clinton's economists would have us believe that high levels of taxation have no effect on the economy. But this is a view from the academic ivory tower. What real-life person out there in the workforce would agree with their theory? Not only does it defy common sense, it defies our daily experience. Americans know far better than any economist that living standards are stagnant at best and declining for many.

This is confirmed by no less an authority than Bill Clinton's own Secretary of Labor, Robert Reich: "Wages for most Americans," he told a House committee last year, "have been stuck and for some have fallen. More and more of them have lost their grip on the middle class or their hope of entering the middle class."

Meanwhile, real median family income has grown by zero percent under the Clinton Administration. For most Americans a single breadwinner was once enough to provide a decent standard of living for their families when they were children. Today, it is all but impossible for most families to provide adequately for their children on fewer than two incomes.

Very few of the children of the Baby Boom generation expect to live as well as their parents—an extraordinary change from the previous 200 years of American history when all Americans expected to live better than their parents, and for their children to live better than they did.

The Clinton Administration would have us believe that the 2.4 percent growth rate they have presided over is the best America can do. In one sense they're right: Given the enormous burden of taxation, regulation and government spending that they have imposed on our economy, 2.4 percent is surprisingly high.

But why live under such a burden? Why accept massive taxes and regulation, as if we had no alternative? Our economic future isn't a matter of chance—it's a matter of choice.

With the Dole-Kemp plan for economic growth, we are offering America a choice. We don't *have* to pay 40 percent or more of our income to government. We don't *have* to accept stagnant wages, low growth, and high interest rates as immutable facts of life. We don't *have* to lower our expectations for the economy—we just need to raise our expectations of government by demanding that government honors, instead of punishes, our efforts.

CHAPTER 7

GOLDEN PROMISES, LACKLUSTER RESULTS:
The Clinton Economic Record

The solution to stagnant wages is not a "grow slow" policy, a policy guided, charted, and controlled by government planners. The solution is faster economic growth, pure and simple. The solution is putting our trust in people, not government.

After all, great economies like America's do not grow according to some official timetable issued by government. They have a life of their own. They follow their own natural dynamic.

The Clinton Administration speaks of our meager 2.4 percent growth rate as the best we can do, as if that rate were fixed in the stars and beyond our power to change. But the truth is America *can* do better, much better, just as we have done many times before. There is no reason in heaven or on earth why our wages and standard of living must be stuck at their present levels. There is no reason wages cannot keep pace with the drive, hope, ambition, and potential of the American workforce.

"Grow slow" is the prescription of Washington economists who, from their "think tanks" and government offices, are under the illusion that they control the American economy. But they don't. Our economy is, and has always been, driven by ideas, the energies, and dreams of the people themselves.

THE "GROW SLOW" SOCIETY

There's no good reason for today's slow growth, but there are plenty of explanations for it. In a way, no one has made a better case for tax cuts than the Clinton Administration. The record Clinton tax increase stifled growth instead of stimulating it.

Let's take a closer look at the American economy four years into the Clinton presidency. The official reports and press releases from Washington could hardly be more glowing. The Clinton Administration claims we have the strongest economy in thirty years. But if that is true, why are Americans working longer and harder and taking home less? Why are wages stagnant? Why are so many families anxious about their future?

Viewed from the most optimistic angle, the good news is that so far, inflation has been stable and interest rates have been relatively low.

The bad news is that the slow rate of growth under President Clinton is almost unprecedented for an economic expansion. The paltry 2.4 percent rate of growth accounts for the stagnant wages, the depressed standard of living, and the general anxiety most Americans feel about their jobs and the future.

Bill Clinton was elected on a promise of a middle-class tax cut. As president he promptly broke his promise and imposed the largest tax *increase* in American history. Not coincidentally, every year since then has brought lower growth. Economic growth today has fallen to new historic lows compared with past periods of expansion. If you were to trace our productivity growth—the key measure of whether wages will grow—on a graph, you would see a nearly perfect flat line running from 1993 to the present. Under President Clinton, U.S. productivity growth has averaged *only 0.4 percentage points per year, or less than half of that in the previous 12 years.*

CLINTON'S ECONOMIC GROWTH GAP

In 1992, President Clinton said that economic growth was the worst it had been in decades. Although he inherited a recovering economy, he said, "We can do better!" What actually happened can be seen in the chart below.

Growth of our economy under his stewardship is worse than the growth he complained about in 1992. In fact, under Bill Clinton, our economy is growing slower than the average growth of the 1980s, slower than post–World War II growth, and slower than each of the last five economic expansions.

THE CLINTON GROWTH GAP

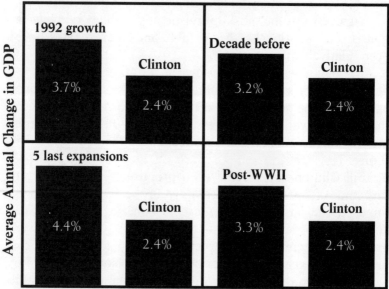

Sources: Department of Commerce, NBER, and JEC calculations.

SLOWEST EXPANSON IN MORE THAN A CENTURY

Just how slow is the American economy growing? Take a look below. This chart comes to us courtesy of the Clinton Administration's Commerce Department:

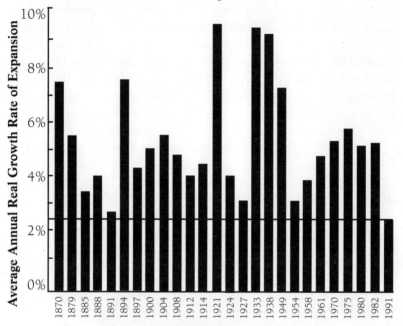

Year expansion started

Sources: Department of Commerce; JEC "Liberating America's Economy," July 1996.

What it shows is that our economy under Bill Clinton is lagging nearly two percentage points behind previous standards. Throughout our history, in every period of economic expansion, the American economy grew at a faster rate than today. We are seeing the slowest expansion of our economy in more than a century.

THE CLINTON TAX AND THE FAMILY BUDGET

The previous charts capture what economists would call the "macro-economic" picture of America today—the broad picture, of stunningly low growth. But for the micro-economic picture to see how that growth rate is felt in the homes of America's families, we have to look at the average family budget. Wages are stuck, productivity is down—but one thing is up: The family tax bill.

Amazingly, the average American family now spends more money on federal, state, and local taxes than on food, clothing, and shelter combined. Federal taxes alone account for more of a family's budget than food, clothing, and medical care combined.

President Clinton calls this "putting people first." We call it putting *government* first. If there is any one "Exhibit A" in the case against the Clinton tax increase of 1993, surely this is it. Our own government is taxing from the families of America more of their own hard-earned money than they spend on the essentials of life.

Here is the exact breakdown:

TAXES DOMINATE A FAMILY'S BUDGET: 1995 BUDGET FOR A TWO-INCOME FAMILY

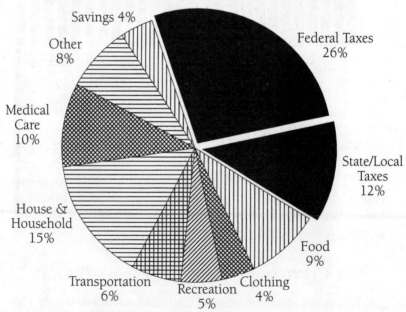

Sources: Tax Foundation; JEC (segments do not total 100% due to rounding).

INDEPENDENCE DAY

Tax Freedom Day marks the point in the year when the average American has earned enough money to finish paying his or her annual tax burden. Everything we earn after that day, we get to keep for ourselves and our families. Until then, we work for the government.

Tax Freedom Day has generally moved later and later in the calendar since World War II. But during the early 1980s, the date stabilized. In 1985, it even moved backward as taxes went down and Americans were allowed to keep more of their own money.

In 1996, Tax Freedom Day was *May 7*—the latest ever. In other words, even as wages are stagnating under the Clinton Administration, tax freedom is receding into the distance. *You're working, on average, the first 127 days of the year just to pay your federal taxes.*

TAX FREEDOM DAY IS LATEST DAY EVER

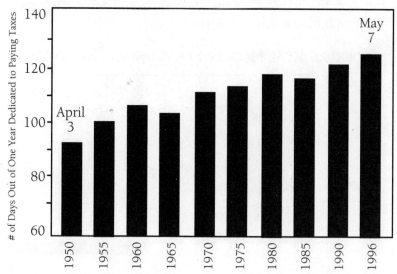

Sources: Tax Foundation; JEC.

This chart does not even take into account state and local taxes. When those are included, the average American is working until early June of every year before the tax collector is satisfied.

How many working parents in today's economy believe they have enough free time to spend with their children? How much more time *could* a mother or father spend with their kids if they didn't have to pay nearly 40 percent of the family income to government?

According to the Census Bureau, the answer is deeply troubling. Under today's economic conditions, the average working mother spends *as many* hours working to pay taxes as she spends with her own children.

HOURLY WAGES: DOWN

During the economic boom of the 1980s, hourly compensation jumped 5.6 percent. In the Clinton years, real hourly wages are declining. Weak economic growth hits hardest on middle-income working Americans, who depend on wage and benefit increases to maintain their standards of living. The graph below tells the story:

WORKERS' REAL HOURLY COMPENSATION STAGNATES

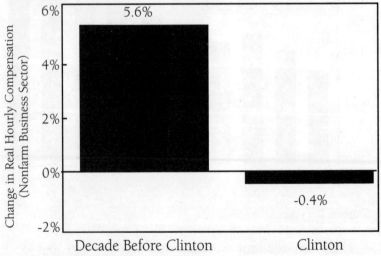

Sources: Bureau of Labor Statistics; JEC.

FAMILY INCOME: DOWN

With wages down, it's no surprise that average family incomes have fallen under the Clinton Administration. From 1983 to 1992, household incomes averaged $33,119. But under Bill Clinton, incomes dropped to $32,153.

REAL MEDIAN HOUSEHOLD INCOME STAGNATES

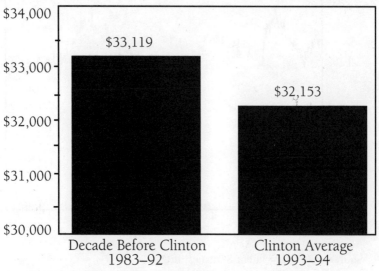

Sources: United States Census Bureau; JEC.

JOB LOCK

When he campaigned in 1992, Bill Clinton expressed concern for the problem of workers who could not leave their jobs for fear of not being able to find another job. How has the Clinton Administration helped solve the problem?

The graph below provides a sure signal that the problem has not been solved. As an economy improves, more people tend to voluntarily leave their jobs in search of better opportunities. During the Reagan years, the number of people willing to leave one job in search of another job rose higher and higher. But not today:

JOB LOCK: VOLUNTARY JOB LEAVERS AS A SHARE OF UNEMPLOYED

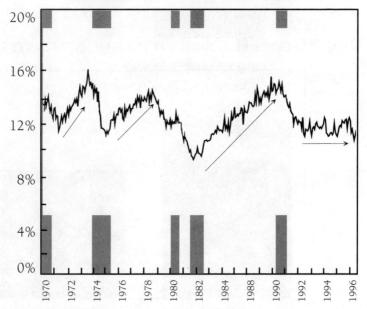

Sources: Bureau of Labor Statistics; JEC.

PRODUCTIVITY: DOWN

Productivity is the amount of goods and services produced by each worker on average throughout the economy. Increasing productivity is the key to attaining higher wages, benefits, and living standards. What are the figures on productivity during the Clinton years? Down—and falling. Productivity growth has all but come to a halt under the Clinton tax policies (see top of next page).

Under Bill Clinton, the average annual growth rate of productivity is just 0.3 percent. Productivity, in other words, is growing slower during this expansion than during any other in recent history.

PRODUCTIVITY PROBLEMS UNDER CLINTON

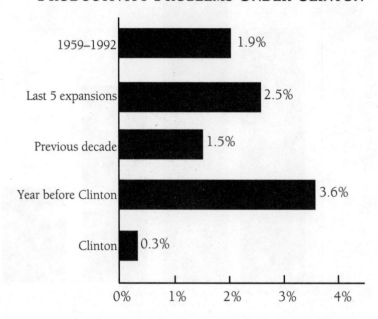

Average annual percent change in nonfarm business sector productivity

Sources: Bureau of Labor Statistics; JEC.

INVESTMENT: WEAK

Investment is the key to economic growth because it allows firms to boost production, create jobs, raise wages, and expand their business. Under Bill Clinton, net investment has been almost 2 percentage points of GDP lower than during the last five expansions—and 1.5 percentage points lower than the previous 30 years.

NET PRIVATE INVESTMENTS STAGNATES

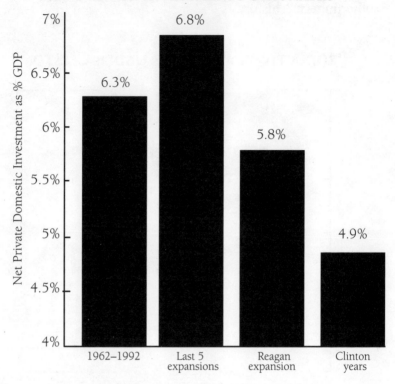

Sources: Bureau of Economic Analysis; JEC.

INTEREST RATES: RISING

Higher interest rates force American families to pay more for home mortgages, car loans, and student loans. When the Republicans took control of Congress in November 1994, interest rates dropped as investors anticipated lower taxes, less federal spending, and a balanced budget.

Congressional Republicans quickly passed the first balanced budget in a generation—a plan that would have saved the typical American family hundreds of dollars a year in lower interest expenses. The president's response? Just as quickly, President Clinton vetoed that balanced budget.

The graph below, based on Treasury Department numbers, traces Clinton policy and the rise and fall of interest rates:

PATH OF INTEREST RATES

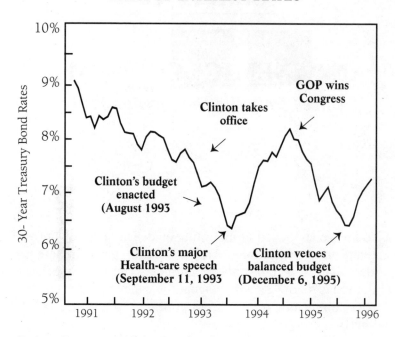

Sources: Department of the Treasury; JEC.

CHAPTER 8

AN "ANEMIC" ECONOMY:
Voices from the Democratic Party

So far we've looked at mounting evidence of serious problems in our economy. And it's worth pausing here to notice that it is not only Republicans who are worried about today's slow-growth, stagnant-wage, high-tax economy. Anxiety about our future is not confined to any one political party.

President Clinton has assured America that "We have the most solid economy in a generation." But why then are both parents in so many families across America forced to take jobs, when one income used to be enough to make ends meet? Why is productivity down, investment down, and the hourly wage stuck?

Many Democrats are wondering the same thing. Even among President Clinton's fellow party leaders, there seems to be growing doubts about Clintonomics. In the best non-partisan tradition of American politics, some unexpected voices have been heard lately warning about the future of American families under their growing burdens:

" . . . we have an anemic rate of economic growth. Mr. President, 2 or 2.3 percent economic growth is not the kind of economic growth that is going to provide the opportunity and the jobs that the American people need and deserve."

—Senator Byron Dorgan (D-SD)
The Congressional Record, *June 20, 1996*

"Right now 16 percent of our workforce does not earn enough to keep a family of four out of poverty. We are seeing a shocking increase in the working poor, the number of people who are working who are in poverty."

—Clinton Secretary of Labor Robert Reich
Testimony before the Joint Economic Committee,
February 22, 1995

"People ask a lot of times, and I read articles, about why in America today with our seemingly wonderful economy that the stores are full of goods, and prices in most cases are pretty decent, why is it that there seems to be this unrest among the American people?"

—Senator Tom Harkin (D-IA)
The Congressional Record, *June 13, 1996*

"Even though some Clinton Administration economic advisers have begun to highlight certain positive economic news . . . it is still true that for many, especially low and moderate income working people, the economic recovery is spotty, partial, and has failed to increase their real take-home pay."

—Senator Paul Wellstone (D-MN)
The Congressional Record, *May 2, 1996*

"We have had growth. It has been comparatively about a C average. If we are happy with a C average in America, fine. I am not. I believe we can do a B or an A in America. I believe our workers can be more productive . . . We have heard it time and time again—that somehow we have reached our limits of growth in America. I do not buy that for a minute. And I do not buy it—that we can only grow 2 or 2.5 percent when there are so many indicators out there that we can grow at 3 or 3.5 maybe as much as 4 percent for a sustained period of time."

—Senator Tom Harkin (D-IA)
The Congressional Record, *June 20, 1996*

"It's hard to make it for a family with two wage earners or three wage earners. Sometimes these families I talk to, they're taking three jobs between two parents. They're taking another part-time job. They're not even seeing their kids, they're working so hard. You know, people say that a lot of people in this country are not working hard. That is absolutely wrong. People in this country are working hard. They're working harder than they've ever worked before."

—Clinton Secretary of Labor Robert Reich
Testimony before the Joint Economic Committee,
February 22, 1995

"While the statistics I have outlined show a strong economy, when I go home I hear a lot of anxiety from farmers, small businesspeople, and families just trying to make a living wage. In fact, wages have stagnated for many middle-class working families. Every year it seems harder and harder to make ends meet."

—Senate Minority Leader Thomas Daschle (D-SD)
The Congressional Record, *June 20, 1996*

"There are a lot of workers out there now who have been discouraged because of downsizing. They are discouraged because of wage stagnation. I see it in my own family, my relatives, who are working at manufacturing jobs. They are discouraged. . . . "

—Senator Tom Harkin (D-IA)
The Congressional Record, *June 20, 1996*

"People in Minnesota and around the country have to just be scratching their heads and wondering what's going on here. Ten blocks from here, why do we not go out and ask whether or not they think we have full employment. Just ask them. This (rate) does not measure subemployment, it does not measure the 1 million discouraged workers, it does not measure people who are working part time because they can not work full time . . . it does not measure all the people who have jobs but not jobs they can count on."

—Senator Paul Wellstone (D-MN)
The Congressional Record, *June 20, 1996*

"Millions of low-wage Americans are working long hours, sometimes two shifts, at difficult, dirty, often dangerous jobs, struggling against enormous barriers to earn a better life for themselves and their families. They are janitors, maids, child care workers, waiters, cashiers, garment workers, fast-food cooks, assemblers, and gas station attendants, doing what needs to be done to make our economy function. These indispensable workers are working harder than ever before and playing by the rules, but are still barely making it financially. They are people who, despite their best efforts, are sometimes dangerously close to having to go on welfare. These are people who hope their kids don't get sick, that their rent or utility bills don't go up, because they don't have an inch of financial slack."

—Clinton Secretary of Labor Robert Reich
Testimony before the Senate Labor and Human
Resources Committee, December 15, 1995

"As economic insecurity multiplies, other values suffer. Community and family feel the pressure. Parents work longer hours or take second jobs, and every extra hour on the job is taking away from their children—time not spent at Little League, or PTA or simply reading a bedtime story."

—Senator Thomas Daschle (D-SD)
The Congressional Record, *February 8, 1996*

CHAPTER 9

FREEDOM AND RESPONSIBILITY:

How to Cut Taxes and Balance the Budget

The Dole-Kemp Economic Growth Plan comes with the most detailed accounting of how we would cut taxes and balance the budget of any presidential campaign in history.

We have to balance the federal budget. We can't wait any longer. In 1995, the federal government paid over $230 billion in interest on the national debt. Nearly 40 cents of every dollar the federal government collects in personal income taxes goes to pay interest on the national debt.

This is unconscionable. We simply cannot continue to mortgage America's future.

The Republican Congress passed two balanced budget plans that provided substantial tax relief for America's families and small businesses. Mr. Clinton enjoys the distinction of being the only president in a generation to veto a balanced budget passed by Congress. And he did so not once, but twice—a double whammy on American families. With a Republican Congress, balancing the budget and providing tax relief are merely a matter of presidential will. If you have it, you can do it. Bob Dole and Jack Kemp have it and we will do it.

THE DOLE-KEMP PLAN BALANCES THE BUDGET

It is extremely difficult to balance a budget in a stagnant economy. Strong economic growth makes balancing the budget easier. The more our economy grows and flourishes, the bigger the tax revenue base. What makes the economy grow? Investment, job creation, new businesses. And to achieve those *we need to lower tax rates* on investment, savings, and entrepreneurship.

Will it work? Leading economists say it will:

- *Gary Becker, a winner of the Nobel Prize for his work in economics, said that the Dole-Kemp Economic Growth Plan "is a bold one and a doable one that can raise the growth rate of the economy over the next few years to well over 3 percent. . . . Now some critics are already calling this 'voodoo economics.' To me, however, it's basically Economics 101. That is what we teach all freshmen, that investors and workers and everybody else in the economy responds in an important way to incentives, including tax incentives."*
- *James M. Buchanan, another Nobel Prize–winning economist, has said: "I support the central thesis in the Dole Economic Growth Plan, which is actually quite different from media reports. . . . I support enthusiastically the emphasis on the need for a Balanced Budget Amendment to the Constitution. And I also support reforms aimed at reducing the intrusiveness of the IRS, and reforms in tort law. I support any and all changes in taxation that will both (1) reduce the aggregate level of taxation, and (2) move the system toward a flat-tax, uniform rate structure."*

Not only Nobel Prize–winning economists agree with the plan; it is also supported by a wealth of experience. For one thing, throughout America today, such reforms *are* being done. Balanced budgets and tax cuts *are* being achieved in statehouses from Boston to Phoenix, from Trenton to Lansing. The results are so impressive that they warrant another chapter below.

Second, there is the example of the Reagan years. Though much maligned by liberal critics since then, President Reagan's across-the-board tax cuts brought about the single largest peacetime expansion in our economy *ever.* Revenues exploded. There was just one problem: For every dollar of that revenue, the then–Democrat-controlled Congress spent $1.33. That is why America was left with the deficits still with us today.

THE DOLE-KEMP TAX CUT: PAID IN FULL

The experience of the eighties taught America a big lesson: Make sure that new revenue goes to balancing the budget, not to *new* federal spending programs. Hold Congress to its word. Make Washington live by its promises by restraining spending through a balanced budget.

The Dole-Kemp plan does that (1) with a credible, year-by-year spending schedule moving us to a balanced federal budget by the year 2002; and (2) by enshrining a balanced budget into law through a Balanced Budget Amendment to the Constitution.

Right up until November, we'll hear the critics say that our tax cut will "blow a hole in the deficit." Naysayers will insist that the Dole-Kemp plan requires draconian cuts in America's social safety net. Such accusations are a sign of weakness in the opposition: They don't have arguments, so they resort to fear.

Of course, many of those critics don't believe in a balanced budget in the first place. The Dole-Kemp plan, however, is based on the balanced budget passed by Congress this past June.

- *The balanced budget plan passed by Congress does not touch Social Security.*
- *The balanced budget plan passed by Congress increases Medicare spending for seniors, from $5,200 to $7,000 per person by the year 2002.*

The balanced budget plan would save Americans $393 billion, including reforms in welfare. And remember this: The Dole-Kemp economic plan does not "cut" overall spending from current levels. The fact is, spending will be 12 percent higher in 2002. In a growing economy, we won't have to cut any of our vital programs to balance the budget. All we do need to do is restrain the *rate* of spending increases.

It can be done—and the Dole-Kemp plan includes the numbers to prove it.

THE DOLE-KEMP PLAN:
A BALANCED BUDGET AND TAX RELIEF

TAX RELIEF	Revenue Loss	Offsets to Revenue Loss
Dole-Kemp Tax Plan	$548 Billion	
GOVERNMENT SAVINGS		
Tax relief already included in Congressional Balanced Budget Plan		$122 billion
Income Growth		$147 billion
Updating the CBO Baseline		$80 billion
Federal Spending Control[1]		$110 billion
FCC Spectrum Auction		$34 billion
Additional Savings and Reform Measures[1]		$55 billion
TOTAL		**$548 billion**
Government Revenue Loss from Tax Plan		**$548 billion**
Government Savings		**$548 billion**
TOTAL FEDERAL DEFICIT IN 2002		**$0.00**

[1] Does not include any reduction in Social Security, Medicare, or Defense programs.

GETTING TO A BALANCED BUDGET

The goal of the Dole-Kemp plan is to provide tax relief to Americans and balance the budget by the year 2002. Our plan incorporates the savings contained in the balanced budget plan passed by Congress in June. The additional savings do not rely on any reduction in Social Security, Medicare, or Defense programs. Instead, this amount comprises savings from three categories: federal spending control, the FCC spectrum auction, and additional savings and reform measures.

Together, these three categories represent $217 billion—about 6 percent of all federal spending, excluding Social Security, Medicare, and Defense programs. In other words, 6 cents on every dollar. A recent "Special Report" by the nonpartisan Tax Foundation called this type of spending restraint "plausible, even minor." The additional savings in these three categories, plus the savings in Congress's June budget resolution, are enough to both balance the budget and finance the tax reduction.

The chart on page 58 illustrates how we can finance the tax reductions. As you can see, the numbers add up. Let's take each of the categories in the chart in order:

TAX RELIEF INCLUDED IN THE CONGRESSIONAL BALANCED BUDGET PLAN

In June 1996 both the U.S. House of Representatives and the U.S. Senate voted on and adopted a thorough, detailed plan to balance the federal budget by the year 2002. As Senate Majority Leader, Bob Dole voted for the plan and supports its provisions. That balanced budget plan included room for $122 billion in tax relief. These are the tax cuts that, in effect, have already been paid for with spending restraints approved by both Houses of Congress.

INCOME GROWTH

The Dole-Kemp Economic Growth Plan for a balanced budget, tax relief, education reform, regulatory relief, and legal reforms will create faster economic growth. Lower tax rates also reduce what economists call "distortions in behavior"—the steps people take to shield their money from high taxation. Lower tax rates make such behavior distortions less necessary and less desirable and, therefore, raise the level of taxable income in the country.

That is not some abstract theory. As Gary Becker, a Nobel Prize winner in economics, put it, this is elementary economics. Martin Feldstein, president of the National Bureau of Economic Research, says: "The increase in taxable income induced by the tax cut substantially reduces revenue loss."

The Dole-Kemp plan conservatively estimates that its combination of tax cuts, deficit reduction, and key reforms will generate $147 billion in additional revenues. This estimate is in line with the taxable income growth that has historically resulted from tax cuts and similar pro-growth policies. As a consequence, the additional revenue will offset about 27 percent of the cost of the tax cuts included in the Dole-Kemp plan.

UPDATING THE CBO BASELINE

Every budget plan includes projections about how fast the economy will grow in the coming years and what effect that will have on the amount of money that comes into the federal treasury. The revenue and expenditure numbers used in the Dole-Kemp Economic Growth Plan are based on Congressional Budget Office projections. These projections are far more conservative than the estimates used by the Clinton Administration. Every year the CBO forecasts how fast the economy grows and what additional revenue the government will earn as a direct result of economic growth. These projections are part of what is called the "CBO baseline."

Current CBO projections about the American economy

and the federal budget were made early in 1996. But since then, these budget revenue projections have proven to be understated. In fact, federal government revenues are already more than $20 billion higher this year than CBO had projected. The Dole-Kemp plan reasonably assumes that just over one-half of this amount ($13 billion) represents a permanent addition to the government's revenue base. The Clinton Administration has already updated its baseline to reflect this higher revenue. Based on this new economic data, our "update to the CBO baseline" will, over six years, result in additional revenues to the federal government of *$80 billion*.

FEDERAL SPENDING CONTROL

Over the next six years, the federal government will spend approximately 1.6 *trillion* on so-called "non-defense discretionary spending" programs. The goal of the Dole-Kemp plan is to reduce that spending by $110 billion. As we said earlier, the additional spending restraint does not rely on any reduction in Social Security, Medicare, or Defense programs. Instead, this $110 billion will come from a combination of reductions in administrative costs and personnel, along with federal department consolidation and closure.

Here are some examples of federal spending restraint that will be part of the Dole Administration:

- *The Department of Energy* was originally created to address the energy crisis of the 1970s. But as so often happens in government, the agency long outlived the crisis. Since the Carter years, the DOE bureaucracy has expanded to $16 billion annually. And two-thirds of the DOE's budget is used for defense-related activities. Much of the remaining third of the budget is spent on outdated and wasteful programs such as a program to produce methane gas from "tuna sludge." The Department also has an extravagant staff travel budget, taking mid-level bureaucrats to all points of the globe on the public tab. Federal laboratories that serve a national security mission will be transferred to agencies more appropriate to their mission. The basic science labs will be transferred to the National Science Foundation.

- *The Department of Commerce* has evolved into a loose collection of more than 100 programs. Former Commerce Secretary Robert Mosbacher called the Department "nothing more than a hall closet where you throw in everything that you don't know what to do with." The General Accounting Office (GAO) goes further, reporting that the Department "faces the most complex web of divided authorities" sharing its "missions with at least 71 federal departments, agencies, and offices." Its bureaucracy is bloated, its infrastructure in disrepair, and more than 60 percent of its budget is dedicated to activities unrelated to commerce.

Under our plan, those programs and functions—like the Advanced Technology Program (a corporate welfare program) and the Economic Development Administration—that are deemed unnecessary, duplicative, or wasteful will be ended entirely. Those remaining programs—the ones actually related to commerce, or to useful activities like census data collection and weather and oceanic research—will be consolidated, reassigned to other appropriate departments, or left to the private sector.

- *Downsizing Administrative and Personnel Costs.* Our federal government will spend tens of billions of dollars over the next six years on administration, overhead, and personnel expenditures. Hundreds of billions of dollars will be spent just on administrative overhead. Virtually every employer and employee in America knows that it is possible to cut overhead expenses. In the real world inhabited by the entrepreneurs and workers in America, cutting overhead is crucial to success. A Dole Administration will bring the same fiscal discipline to federal bureaucracies.

FCC SPECTRUM AUCTION

The federal government currently owns and leases part of the spectrum—the word specialists use to describe our public airwaves. But broadcasters use it for free. Under other circumstances, many in our media would call this a "government giveaway" or a costly instance of corporate welfare. And they'd be right: The broadcast industry makes billions upon billions of dollars using the public airwaves, while the public is getting exactly nothing. Reasonable estimates conclude that the sale of further portions of the spectrum to the broadcast and telecommunications industry would generate approximately $34 billion in receipts for the government.

ADDITIONAL SAVINGS AND REFORM MEASURES

The Dole-Kemp plan is premised on changing the way government works across-the-board. Cutting tax rates across-the-board is just one part of the Dole-Kemp vision. Our plan makes conservative estimates about the amount of money that can be saved simply by making some common sense reforms. Below we list just a few illustrative examples of the type of reforms that could put us on the road to achieving the desired level of savings:

- *The Line-Item Veto.* After many attempts, the Republican Congress succeeded last year in enacting this fundamental reform. Under the new law, the President may strike particular expenditures from the federal budget, instead of being forced to sign or veto the budget as a whole. Under a Dole

Administration, that line-item veto will be used to its full extent in defense of the taxpayers of America.

* *Closing Corporate Loopholes, Customs Legal Reform, and Tax Amnesty.* If there was ever a time when some corporations needed special breaks or favors from Congress, that time is over. Least of all, should government be giving special breaks to corporations when working families and small businesses enjoy no such favors? Closing such loopholes will save money and restore fairness to the system. As with the tax rate reductions, closing corporate loopholes is consistent with fundamental tax reform. The Dole-Kemp reforms will also more closely monitor the valuation of imports to ensure that foreign firms are fully complying with existing U.S. customs law.

  As part of a transition to a new tax system, the Dole-Kemp plan envisions a limited amnesty period during which individuals and businesses can voluntarily pay their back taxes and interest without penalty or fear of civil or criminal prosecution. The federal government, however, has never had an amnesty program. But thirty-five states have raised well over $1.5 billion in additional revenue. Connecticut, for example, with a population of 3.3 million people has collected more than $100 million in back taxes during its amnesty period.

* *Program Reforms.* Many federal programs are in need of reform. Some make payments to people who don't qualify or don't deserve them. For example, President Clinton's own budget documents estimate that there is $1.7 billion annually in overpayments due to fraud and errors in the food stamp program. If the Clinton Administration can't do anything about it, a Dole Administration will. In addition, charges for traditional government

programs that benefit corporations—such as trade-mark services—have recently expired and should be extended. These extensions were part of the Congressional balanced budget plan passed in June.

- *Net Interest Savings.* When the Dole-Kemp plan is enacted into law and the budget is balanced, the federal government will borrow less money in the credit markets. By reducing borrowing the federal government has a net interest saving. All budget reduction bills that have recently passed Congress have included an estimate of net interest savings.

CHAPTER 10

THE REAGAN LEGACY:
Lower Taxes, Soaring Growth

President Clinton and his administration have compared our economic growth initiative to the policies of President Reagan. They mean it as an insult. We take it as a compliment.

Of course, things are different now from when Ronald Reagan was President. Back then, the Democratic Congress refused to put a lid on government spending. But with a Republican Congress and a Republican President, we will keep federal spending in check and provide tax relief to American taxpayers.

REMEMBER CARTER'S "MALAISE"?

Let's get a few other things straight about the Reagan legacy. Most Americans remember the Reagan years as a time of growth and expanding opportunity in America. If that's how you recall the Reagan era, there's a good reason for it: That's what it was—a time of unprecedented growth in the American economy.

When Ronald Reagan ran for President in 1980, America was in an economic "malaise." Under President Carter, America faced double-digit interest rates, double-digit inflation, and no sign of prosperity in sight. Economists even had to invent a new word to describe America's condition— "stagflation."

"STAGFLATION"

The inflation rate under Carter reached 12 percent per year. Unindexed tax rates—which pushed middle- and lower-income families into tax brackets previously reserved for the rich—made the problem of inflation even worse. The prime interest rate hit 15 percent. From 1979 to 1980, real median income dropped from over $38,000 to just under $36,000. In fact, one of the sharpest declines in median-family income on record occurred in 1980. Federal regulation of our economy tightened.

And like today, each problem fed on the other: High taxes smothered any incentive for Americans to save or invest. Declining savings led to a drop in production. Falling productivity led to stagnant wages. And so on, in the same sad chain of cause-and-effect we're seeing in today's low-growth economy.

WHAT REALLY HAPPENED DURING THE 1980s?

The Clinton Administration has been trying to rewrite history. They want us to remember the 1980s as a period of despair and economic failure. Unfortunately for them, the historical record tells the exact opposite. The Reagan economic boom was the longest peacetime expansion in our nation's history. It was a period of sustained prosperity and growth—growth that we wish we could achieve today. It is important to understand what *really* happened to the economy during the 1980s. The truth is, by every objective standard of economic health, the 1980s brought good news to American taxpayers and families.

THE REAGAN TAX CUTS

President Reagan cut income tax rates across the board. Critics said it couldn't be done. But Ronald Reagan did it with the help of Bob Dole and Jack Kemp in Congress. President Reagan reduced the regulatory burden on American businesses. He reversed inflation with a sound monetary policy leading to low inflation and declining interest rates. What followed? The longest peacetime expansion of our economy in history.

ECONOMIC GROWTH

Following the Reagan tax cuts, from 1983 to 1989, allowing for inflation, the entire American economy grew by 31 percent. America's economic growth averaged 3.9 percent per year. That stands up pretty well against the 2.4 percent average annual-growth rate our current president calls the best we can do. If that's the best America can do, why did we do so much better under Ronald Reagan's leadership?

What about new jobs? In the Reagan expansion years our economy produced nearly *20 million new jobs.*

FAMILY INCOMES

Under President Reagan's stewardship, our economy not only produced jobs—but jobs with better pay. Reagan's detractors concede those 20 million jobs but insist they were low-paying jobs. False. From 1983 to 1989, real-median family income rose 1.7 percent *per year.* That's far better than today's zero growth in median-family income.

PRODUCTIVITY

For real wages to rise, productivity must rise. Over the past 30 years there has been a general decline in U.S. productivity. Under President Reagan, productivity *rose* at a 1.6 percent annual rate from 1983 to 1989. Productivity under Mr. Clinton's economic policies? Exactly 0.4 percent annually.

SAVINGS

Under Reagan, gross private savings were 17.2 percent of GDP between 1983–89. Under President Clinton, the savings rate has declined to 14.6 percent of GDP.

By nearly every measure, the American economy was stronger in the 1980s than it is today. There was no secret to Ronald Reagan's policies. They were simply based on a belief in the American people themselves. Ronald Reagan believed that if only government got out of the way and unleashed the talents and genius of the people, they would do the rest. And as the record shows, they did.

THE RISING TIDE

No graph captures the story of the Reagan years better than the one on page 70. It dispenses once and for all with the class warfare charges that only the rich gained during the 1980s.

As you can see, when taxes are low and the economy is strong—as they were during the 1980s—*all* Americans benefitted. The rich did better, but so did the poor and the middle class—every American income bracket saw its wealth rise.

But when taxes are high and growth is slow—as they have been during the 1990s—only the top income earners get ahead. The poor and the middle class are the ones who see their incomes fall. High taxes lock people in place and stifle upward mobility. Low taxes create a dynamic economic environment where everyone has a chance to move ahead.

REAGANOMICS: A RISING TIDE LIFTED ALL BOATS

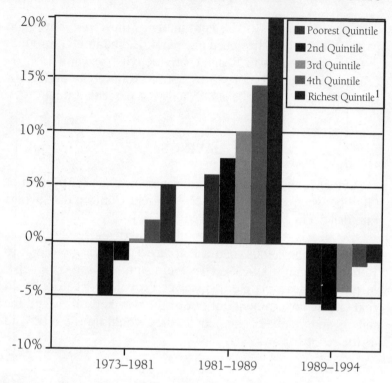

[1]Richest quintile refers to top 5 percent.
Source: CATO Institute, based on: U.S. Bureau of Census.

Economists divide Americans into "quintiles." From 1981 to 1989 every income quintile—from the richest to the poorest—saw an increase in real income. The average real income of those in the bottom quintile of households increased from $7,954 to $8,391. The income of those in the second lowest quintile rose from $18,856 to $20,797.

The rich, in fact, ended up paying a *larger* proportion of the total tax burden even under lower marginal rates. As the next chart shows, the share of total taxes paid by the top 1 percent of all taxpayers increased from 17.6 percent in 1981 to *27.5 percent* in 1988. For the top 5 percent of all taxpayers, the tax share rose from 36 percent in 1981 to 46 percent in

1988. Meanwhile, the middle-class tax burden declined *from 57.5 percent to 48.7 percent.*

RICH PAY GREATER SHARE OF INCOME TAX BURDEN AFTER REAGAN TAX CUTS

Percent of Total Personal Income Taxes Paid

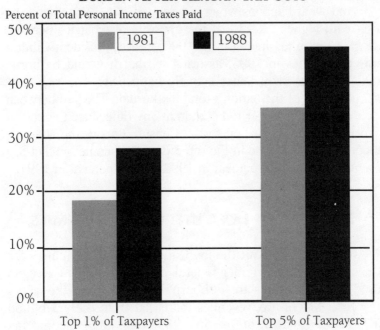

Source: Tax Foundation.

How can this be? Lower tax rates discourage tax avoidance. Less money goes into tax shelters and more money goes into productive investments that make our economy grow. That expands the tax base.

Far from being some new theory of economics, this is what John F. Kennedy meant in 1962 when he said:

"It is a paradoxical truth that the tax rates are too high today and tax revenues are too low; and the soundest way to raise revenues in the long run is to cut taxes now. The purpose of cutting taxes now is not to incur a budget deficit, but to achieve the more prosperous, expanding economy which can bring a budget surplus."

Acting on this conviction, President Kennedy lowered the highest tax rates from 91 percent to 70 percent. The result was just as he predicted. From 1963 to 1966, tax revenues actually rose by 16 percent. For those earning $50,000 or more tax collection rose by 57 percent.

And what happens when government sets out to soak the rich with higher taxes? Just the opposite of what it intended, as the Clinton tax increases of 1993 proved. President Clinton raised tax rates in 1993, assuring us that it would be borne mainly by the rich. What actually happened? The rich now shoulder less of the nation's total tax burden. The gap between rich and poor is larger today than at any time since the end of World War II. According to the Census Bureau, the share of income going to those in the top 5 percent income bracket has *increased* from 18.6 percent in 1992 to 21.2 percent in 1994.

THE REAGAN TAX CUTS: RISING REVENUES

Finally, what about the myth that Reagan's tax cuts were the cause of our terrible federal deficit? President Reagan used to say that facts are stubborn things. Here are the facts:

Total federal tax revenues increased from $599.3 billion in 1981 to *$990.7 billion* in 1989. Individual income tax revenues increased from $285.9 billion in 1981 to *$445.7 billion* in 1989—a 56 percent increase.

But, during the 1980s, federal spending under a Democrat-controlled Congress increased 69 percent. It rose from $678.2 billion in 1981—to $1.14 trillion in 1989. The following figures demonstrate that out-of-control spending was the primary cause of an expanding federal deficit during this period.

As a matter of fact, federal tax revenues increased faster after Reagan's *tax cuts* than they have following the two *tax increases* of the 1990s. Income tax revenues, after adjusting for inflation, increased 2.2 percent per year from 1981 to 1989. And that was after a 25 percent, across-the-board tax cut. But from 1990 to 1995, tax revenues increased just 1.34 percent.

FEDERAL RECEIPTS AND SPENDING (1981–1995)

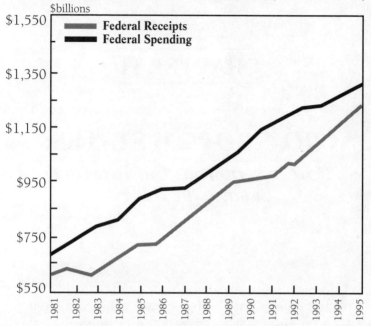

Source: Office of Management and Budget.

That's after the top tax rate was increased dramatically, and after the single largest tax increase in our history.

The lesson: Tax increases don't help the government raise money. They simply slow the economy down. And an ebbing tide lowers all boats.

Lower Tax Rates Work:
Revenues Grew Faster Under Kennedy and Reagan

Average Annual Increase in Real Income Tax Revenues

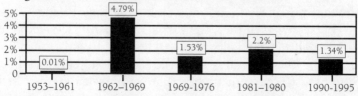

Source: *Budget of the U.S. Government, FY 1997*, Office of Management and Budget.

CHAPTER 11

PRO-GROWTH STATES:
How Governments Cut Taxes and Balance the Budget

" *You can't cut taxes and balance the budget.*" That's the conventional wisdom we're hearing from the Washington elite, just a generation after John F. Kennedy disproved it and ten years after Ronald Reagan disproved it yet again. The media say it. The liberal Democrats in Congress say it. Bill Clinton says it. Faced with these conflicting opinions, we'll side with John F. Kennedy and Ronald Reagan.

But you don't have to rely on history for an example of how to cut taxes and balance budgets. It's being done right now in states across America.

Just last year, twenty-one states enacted tax cuts and every one balanced its budget.

What else is happening in those states? Economic growth by leaps and bounds. Job creation. Rising wages and job security. In fact, the magazine *Business Week* compared high-tax and low-tax states. It found that "job growth in low-tax states over the last eight years has been a stunning 65 percent higher than in high-tax states." It is time Washington learned from the examples set by the states.

Not surprisingly, most of the states seeing this growth have Republican governors. But not all. Far away from Washington, a bipartisan consensus is running squarely against the conventional wisdom that "it can't be done." It's crossing party lines and pointing the way for Washington. Here's the roll call of tax relief, state by state:

NEW YORK

After defeating three-term governor Mario Cuomo, Republican Governor George Pataki cut over $2 billion in state spending. At the same time, Governor Pataki cut state income taxes by a full *20 percent*. At the end of the year, the state's budget was balanced.

PENNSYLVANIA

Republican Governor Tom Ridge was elected in 1994. In 1995, he led a successful fight in the legislature for a $200 million business income tax cut. (As a result of his fiscal discipline, the state is also expected to see government spending *drop* in 1997—the first time that will happen in a quarter century.)

MICHIGAN

Elected in 1990, Republican Governor John Engler has enacted no fewer than 21 tax cuts in six years. According to the conventional wisdom, that should have put Michigan deep in the red. It didn't. The state runs a healthy budget surplus. In addition to a strong economy, Engler led the fight to reform the state's welfare system and bring free choice to the public education system—just as we intend to do in the Dole-Kemp plan.

NEW JERSEY

The critics scoffed when Christine Todd Whitman ran as the Republican candidate for New Jersey governor on a pledge to cut taxes 30 percent in three years. They were only partly right. Governor Whitman kept her tax cut promise, but she did it in *two years* instead of three. With help from a Republican legislature, she balanced the budget in New Jersey while providing $1.2 billion in tax relief. And the state's revenues? According to the CATO Institute, which completed a fiscal study of state budgets, revenues are growing more quickly under Governor Whitman's tax cut agenda than under her predecessor, a Democrat, who gave New Jersey the biggest tax increase in its history.

WISCONSIN

Republican Governor Tommy Thompson is best known for his bold reforms in welfare and education. But he's also cut the state's income tax rates, reduced the capital gains tax, slashed property taxes by more than $1 billion, and almost done away entirely with the state's inheritance tax. All of this has been achieved while balancing the budget every year.

ARIZONA

Under Republican leadership, Arizona has cut taxes five years running, and even proposes eliminating the state income tax altogether. This year alone Governor Fife Symington brought down state tax rates by 20 percent for a total of $2.6 billion in tax cuts. Not only is the budget balanced: Arizona has a surplus of more than $300 million.

NEW HAMPSHIRE

New Hampshire is well known as the state with no sales tax and no income tax. But under Governor Steve Merrill, New Hampshire has cut taxes on business profits, real estate transfers, and eliminated the corporate franchise tax. Result: A balanced budget and growing economy.

MASSACHUSETTS

Republican William Weld was re-elected governor in 1994 by a huge margin, on the strength of a record that includes a cut in state income taxes from 6.25 percent to 5.95 percent. State revenues increased nearly 12 percent over a two-year period.

The chart below offers a few more details on each state:

Tax Rate Changes and Their Impact on Revenue		
State	**Recent Tax Changes**	**1992–94 Revenue Growth**
Arizona	Raised personal exemption and elderly income exemption (1992–93)	+7.9%
Mass.	Cut personal income tax rate from 6.25% to 5.95% (1992)	+11.8%
Michigan	Cut state tax on business (1992)	+3.3%
New Jersey	Doubled top personal income tax rate from 3.5% to 7% (1991, under Democratic Governor Jim Florio)	-6.1%

Sources: National Association of State Budget Officers, *Fiscal Survey of the States*, various editions; National Conference of State Legislatures, *State Tax Actions*, various editions; CATO Institute, 1994.

CHAPTER 12

TAX RELIEF FOR SMALL BUSINESS

Since the days when our parents were small-business owners—the Doles running a small cream-and-egg stand in Russell, Kansas; the Kemps operating their family trucking delivery business in Los Angeles—America has always honored the efforts of the small entrepreneur with big hopes.

But they are not just figures of yesterday: They are today—they have always been—the driving force in our economy. And today they are more important than ever. America's small businesses are the engine of job creation in our economy. Small firms employ one in four American workers. Women now own more than 7.9 million small businesses. In fact, women are starting new businesses at twice the rate of men.

The last thing any government should do is hit those small entrepreneurs with more taxes and regulations than they face already. But that's exactly what our government is doing. If the federal government set out deliberately to thwart small-business owners and their dreams, it could hardly do the job more effectively.

END THE WAR ON SMALL BUSINESS

Perhaps the most devastating blow to small business came with the 1993 Clinton tax. Under that tax, millions of small businesses operating as proprietorships, partnerships, and S Corporations, suddenly were forced to pay at a new and higher *top income tax rate* of 39.6 percent.

Bill Clinton boasts that his economic policies have helped small business. He claims that his tax increase only hit "the rich." Apparently he defines rich as any entrepreneurs creating new jobs, new businesses, and new products. As the chart below shows, *more than two-thirds of the people who pay President Clinton's new top tax rate are America's small business owners.*

CLINTON'S INCOME TAX HIKE ON SMALL BUSINESS

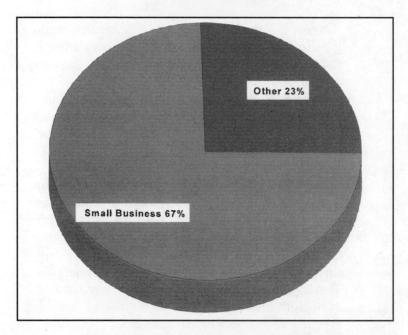

Other 23%

Small Business 67%

Sources: Department of Treasury; JEC.

Around America, suddenly millions of farmers, shop owners, and fledgling businesses found themselves in the same category as multi-millionaires. After President Clinton's tax hike, the local, family-owned Chevrolet dealer discovered that he was in a higher tax bracket than General Motors!

SOCKING IT TO SMALL BUSINESS

Since the 1993 tax increase, President Clinton has persisted in proving that he is no friend of the small-business owner. Time after time, issue after issue, he has made it harder and more costly for America's entrepreneurs to succeed. Although Congress has passed several measures to encourage and help the small-business owner, the president has consistently fought or vetoed these measures. It is a record that should make every small-business owner in the country see red:

- *Opposed Regulatory Reform.* President Clinton threatened to veto legislation that brought sensible risk-assessment and cost-benefit analysis to new regulations.
- *Stifling Regulation.* As of April 1996, the regulations published in the Federal Register had grown to 202 volumes and 131,803 pages. A large portion of these regulations fall right on the back of small and new businesses.
- *Vetoed Product Liability Reform.* With bipartisan support, Congress this year passed a product liability reform bill. This vital piece of legal reform would have directly helped small businesses that often suffer disproportionately in frivolous lawsuits that award millions of dollars to plaintiffs. The legislation would have helped lower the cost of liability insurance, which is a growing cost for every small business in the country.
- *Vetoed Securities Litigation Reform.* With broad

bipartisan support, Congress last year passed by enormous margins a securities litigation reform bill that would have reined in the frivolous, multi-million dollar lawsuits against public companies that disproportionately affected growing high-tech firms. The bill had near-universal support from small computer, software, and bio-tech companies. President Clinton sided with the well-financed trial lawyers lobby and vetoed the bill. Both Republicans and Democrats worked together to override his veto.

- *Vetoed Small Business Tax Cut.* When Congress sent the President the Balanced Budget Act of 1995, it included a host of tax-relief measures for small businesses. These included estate tax reform, capital gains tax rate reductions, increased deductibility of health insurance, and increased equipment expensing. President Clinton vetoed the bill.

- *Opposed Davis-Bacon Repeal.* The Davis-Bacon Act of 1931 discriminates against small business by forcing employers to pay exorbitant "prevailing wage" rates in local areas whenever they participate in federal contracts. This effectively excludes small businesses from competing for these contracts. When legislation emerged in Congress to repeal Davis-Bacon, the president threatened a veto.

- *Ignored Small Business Recommendations.* In June 1995, President Clinton invited 2,000 small business owners to attend the White House Conference on Small Business and asked them to make policy recommendations. According to the House Small Business Committee, the president has since opposed 22 of the its top 26 recommendations. As of June 1996, the president has vetoed ten legislative provisions implementing these recommendations; opposed congressional action on four other recommendations, and, of those recommendations that federal agencies have authority to implement, failed to implement five and only partially implemented three others.

- *Attempted To Reform Health Care By Mandates on Small Business.* The original Clinton health care reform package proposed costly employer mandates as the primary mechanism to implement his national health care plan. Had he succeeded, the plan would have cost employers $42 billion and forced employers to lay off 710,000 workers in the first year. *Forty-three percent of the job loss would occur in businesses that employ fewer than 20 employees.*

LET SMALL BUSINESSES FLOURISH

How can we best help our small businesses? By cutting their tax and regulatory burden. According to David Burton, a tax analyst with the Argus Group, the Dole-Kemp economic plan will reduce the tax liabilities of 19.2 million small businesses by 15 percent.

In practice, that means that a small retailer registered as an S Corporation has a total taxable income of $100,000. Assuming the owner is a married woman with two children, her tax in 1996 would be $13,858. *Our tax reforms would reduce her tax by a full $3,275.*

In addition, the Dole-Kemp plan will:

- *Increase the estate tax exemption for businesses so that family-owned businesses can stay in the family.*
- *Cut the capital gains tax rate in half,* which will help business owners and also unleash capital that will be invested in new and rising small businesses.
- *Restore a meaningful home-office tax deduction to provide relief to the growing number of home-based small businesses.* In general, these millions

of home-based entrepreneurs should be treated as a welcome force in our economy, not treated with suspicion by the IRS.

- *Reform the independent contractor and employee classification rule to make the rules clear, simple, and objective—so that small businesses can easily determine up-front if their new hire is an employee or an independent contractor.*
- *Increase the tax deduction for health insurance costs for self-employed small businesses from 80 percent to 100 percent.*
- *Permit small businesses access to Medical Savings Accounts and other health-care options.*
- *Allow small businesses to set up SIMPLE pension plans, free of burdensome IRS rules.*

The Dole-Kemp economic plan is designed to make the entire economy grow. The only way that can happen is by making sure that small business helps lead the way to years of economic prosperity.

CHAPTER 13

FREEDOM FROM STIFLING REGULATION

Good government and excessive regulation are very different things. Common sense usually recognizes the difference. Like most Americans, we believe government has a duty to protect the life, safety, health, and property of the people. For example, this requires regulations to assure airline safety, prevent pollution of our air and waters, and require accurate labeling of consumer products.

That is just common sense. It is a legitimate and vital function of government. A Dole-Kemp Administration will carry out these regulatory duties to the fullest.

But just as fundamental is the right of the people to be free of needless meddling by government in their economic affairs. It is a careful balance, requiring vigilance by government, but equally a respect for the rights of free people working, risk-taking, and striving to succeed in a free economy.

In a Dole-Kemp Administration, we will bring a long-overdue standard of fairness and common sense to government regulations. Entrepreneurs around America—the folks who make our economy run—should not have to answer to endless decrees from the bureaucratic potentates on the Potomac, who themselves are often exceeding their mandate from Congress. It is time we regulated the regulators.

THE HEAVY COSTS OF REGULATION

Under the Clinton Administration, the number of pages in the Federal Register rose to the third highest of all time in 1993—to about 70,000 pages. Take a look at the chart below:

NUMBER OF PAGES IN THE FEDERAL REGISTER

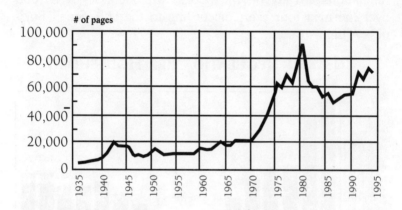

Sources: Marvin Zonis & Associates, Inc.; JEC.

THE HIDDEN TAX OF REGULATION

What exactly is the effect of regulation on our rate of growth, on job creation, and productive enterprises around America? We'll never really know for sure, but it's enormous. One estimate puts the total loss at over a trillion dollars. That's the value of the economic activity squandered each year because of government regulations, according to the Center for the Study of American Business. And even such a staggering figure cannot begin to capture the loss in jobs, take-home pay, and opportunity for America's families.

President Clinton's own administration has estimated that the cost of complying with federal regulations was at least $668 billion in 1995. A more modest estimate. But even if they're right, *that's still larger than the entire personal income tax for that year.*

Viewed from another angle, by the Clinton Administration's own admission, federal regulation costs the average American household *more than $6,000.* By the year 2000, these costs are expected to rise to almost $721 billion, or $7,000 per household.

In other words, even if no new federal regulations were imposed, the "regulatory tax" on each American family, from regulations already on the books, will increase by $1,000 over the next four years, according to the U.S. Small Business Administration.

COSTS OF REGULATION PER HOUSEHOLD

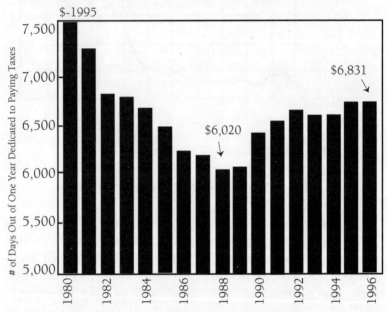

Sources: Thomas B. Hopkins, "Profiles of Regulatory Costs," Report to the SBA, November 1995; JEC

And yet the Clinton Administration has done nothing to lighten that regulatory burden. The burden has grown heavier since 1993. Every time the President has been given a chance to enact serious regulatory reform, he has opposed it or threatened a veto.

He opposed the Comprehensive Regulatory Reform Act of 1995, which would have required cost-benefit and risk-assessment analysis of new federal regulations. He vetoed product-liability reform legislation, which would have reined in trial lawyers. His "Reinventing Government" program mainly looked at internal agency rules, not at those regulations that actually burden individuals and private business.

Meanwhile, his administration has failed to enforce the Paperwork Reduction Act, which requires the government to set a goal of at least a 10 percent annual reduction of the paperwork burden. A Government Accounting Office study estimates that the Clinton Administration will achieve at most a 1 percent reduction in 1996. His administration even exempted the IRS from the Act. In a June 1996 report, the Government Accounting Office stated that since 1989, "the IRS's paperwork burden has accounted for more than three-quarters of the government-wide total."

It is outrageous that the IRS, which imposes so much paperwork on the American people, should be exempted from such a law. Why shouldn't the bureaucrats at the IRS have to live by the same rules as everyone else?

In a Dole-Kemp Administration, regulators will find themselves on the receiving end of some very strict regulations from the White House and Congress. And they'll begin with the IRS. Here's what we intend to do:

AN AGENDA FOR REAL REGULATORY RELIEF

- *Apply a rigorous cost-benefit standard to all new federal regulations.*

Under our administration, no federal regulations shall be imposed unless they can first be justified by sound science and economic good sense. We will establish a system in which every regulation is weighed according to these simple criteria. Only those regulations in which the benefits clearly outweigh the costs will be approved. Individuals and businesses will be able to take federal agencies to court if those agencies ignore this requirement. The small-business owner, farmer, and ordinary citizen will no longer be powerless.

- *Establish a Sunsetting Task Force to review regulations.*

The principle is simple: Federal regulations should not be set in stone. Many of the thousands of regulations now on the books are outdated; they linger on long after their original purpose has been served, at great cost in dollars and grief to the people forced to live by them.

In a Dole-Kemp Administration, we will create a Sunsetting Task Force whose sole mission will be to find those regulations that serve no good purpose. It will recommend the elimination of regulations that are outdated, ineffective, or not cost-efficient. The task force will be co-chaired by the Director of the Office of Management and Budget and the head of the Small Business Administration. We need to get away from the whole bureaucratic mindset which assumes that one group makes the rules and the other group lives by them.

- *Require Periodic Review of All Regulations.*

No federal regulations, except those critical to protecting the lives, safety, and property of the people, should live on indefinitely. The way Washington now works, the burden of proof is always on those who would eliminate a given federal regulation. It should be the other way around. The burden of proof should rest with those who would maintain a regulation. In a Dole-Kemp Administration, all new federal regulations will be reviewed and re-evaluated every four years.

There are many advantages to this process. But one of them is often overlooked: The absence of senseless regulations will inspire a greater respect among the people toward those federal regulations that really are essential.

- *Force every federal agency—including the IRS—to comply with all provisions of the Paperwork Reduction Act.*

Every year the IRS sends out some 8 billion—yes, *billion*—pages of paper in all its endless forms and letters to the taxpayers of America. Laid end to end, that stream of paper would encircle our planet 28 times. We will rescind the Clinton exemption that allows the IRS to avoid compliance with the Paperwork Reduction Act.

Milton Friedman, the renowned Nobel Prize–winning economist, has emphasized the importance of reforming and rolling back regulations as part of a complete plan to boost economic growth. In an article published in the *Wall Street Journal* in 1995, he wrote:

[I]t is hard to avoid the conclusion that dismantling the regulatory state would foster a return to the long-run capacity of the U.S. to grow at roughly 4% a year, and the twin revolutions (technological and political) should enable us to achieve an even higher rate of growth. We have been setting our sights far too low.

CHAPTER 14

MORE CHOICE, BETTER SCHOOLS, AND A WORLD-CLASS WORK FORCE

Education and job-training reform are essential components of our economic plan. The poor performance of our public schools is one reason why real wages have been stagnant in recent years.

We know from experience and common sense that better skills and more know-how are directly tied to higher wages and growing salaries. The Dole-Kemp plan pursues the twin goals of genuine education and job-training reform. First, it will help create the finest schools in the world where parents have a more direct role in the children's education. Second, it will create new opportunities for all Americans—including those in the work force for many years—to acquire the skills that are essential to remaining competitive in a 21st century economy.

WHAT HAPPENED TO OUR SCHOOLS?

Many parents and taxpayers look at the state of our public schools today and ask with a sense of bewilderment, "What on earth *happened*?" Where are the schools that were once a model to the world? Where is the love of learning, the respect for standards, the sense of responsibility and simple decency that once prevailed in our classrooms?

It wasn't long ago when parents in America who couldn't afford a private school, or who sent their kids to the public school by choice, could count on their child learning the basic things. Our schools were never perfect, but they did the job: When you graduated from high school, you knew the basics of math, the language, history, and science. For many of us, a quality public school education was the first big break we had.

And more than that, the best of those schools instilled in generations of Americans some even more important things. For generations, in public schools from Brooklyn to Chicago to Russell, Kansas, children of all classes, races, and creeds were brought together in a common appreciation of America itself. The schools instilled ambition, hope, discipline, decency, and a common love for our country and what it stands for.

America's schools can be that way again. Just as with our low-growth economy, there is no reason why we have to accept mediocre schools as a fact of life. This is a free country—we have choices. Let's start making them by reclaiming our public schools.

In a Dole-Kemp Administration, we're going to do just that. Our reforms of public education will be guided by three simple principles:

- *Individual Responsibility*
- *Parental Control and Choice*
- *Accountability*

RESPONSIBILITY IN THE CLASSROOM

In general, what made our schools great was a faith in freedom—in parents left to make important choices for their own children. It was a system of mutual trust: it trusted parents to make wise decisions; it trusted teachers to put the interests of children before anything else. It was based on shared standards of achievement, and on a faith in children to meet those standards.

Today those simple ideas have too often been abandoned in public education, with troubling and often tragic results. At their best, our public schools can prepare children for life's opportunities, for work, for the duties of citizenship. Today, many of our schools are failing on all three counts:

- Where schools should be instilling hope, drive, and ambition, too often they breed a spirit of apathy and mediocrity.
- Where schools should instill an appreciation of our country and its history, often they seem to reflect a blindness toward America and its finer moments.
- Instead of preparing the next generation to work and thrive in the new economy, often our schools seem mired in trendy education fads of little or no practical value.

THE CLINTON RECORD: LOFTY RHETORIC AND FALLING PERFORMANCE

After four years of high-flown rhetoric from Bill Clinton about "investing in education," what are the results?

- SAT scores remain far too low.
- One of the biggest academic movements in our colleges is remedial education, because millions of high-school graduates arrive on campus unable to solve a simple math problem or write a simple essay.
- And think what it means for the economy when

90 percent of corporate executives in a survey said that one of the most serious problems among younger employees was functional illiteracy.

Meanwhile, those in charge of our schools only seem to grow more complacent as their vise-like monopoly becomes tighter. Too often our schools are run by the dictates of bureaucrats and teachers' unions who seem to regard the schools not as a trust, but as political territory to be guarded at all costs.

In too many instances, the rigid, anti-reform mentality of the teachers' unions stand in the way. When disciplinary codes are proposed, lawsuits are often filed. When academic standards are proposed, the teachers' unions oppose them. When competency tests for teachers are proposed, the unions fight them tooth and nail.

Still worse, in many of our cities the public schools are danger zones. Not only are the classrooms in crisis: Many of America's kids have to walk through metal detectors to get to them. Studies show that over 5,000 teachers are attacked each month in our public schools.

This is our dividend on billions and billions invested in education under Bill Clinton: Low test scores, a higher drop-out rate, massive remedial education, and an illiteracy rate growing by leaps and bounds.

From the teachers' unions and the Clinton Administration, we still hear the claim that American taxpayers aren't investing quite enough in our public schools. If only we pour a few billion more dollars into public education, maybe *that* will do it. But the truth is the problem cannot be solved with money alone. The following numbers lay that criticism to rest:

PUBLIC EXPENDITURES FOR PRIMARY AND SECONDARY EDUCATION (1991–92)

Country	Per Pupil Expenditures (in constant 1992 dollars)
United States	$6,984
Sweden	$5,336
Norway	$5,262
Canada	$4,935
Switzerland	$4,838
Denmark	$4,475
Finland	$4,237
Austria	$4,107
Italy	$4,036
France	$3,630
Belgium	$3,438
United Kingdom	$3,365
Netherlands	$3,192
Japan	$2,707
Australia	$2,532
New Zealand	$2,263
Spain	$2,094
Ireland	$2,083
Hungary	$1,728

Sources: U.S. Department of Education, National Center for Educational Statistics; The Center for Education Reform, 1995.

Far from holding back, no other nation spends as much on education as we do, yet over our public schools hangs an air of failure, frustration, and futility.

ACCOUNTABILITY IN EDUCATION: WHO SPEAKS FOR THE TAXPAYER?

There is only one way to reform our schools: *We must end the teachers unions' chokehold on public education in America.*

America has some of the finest and most dedicated teachers in the world. But let's face it: Every conscientious teacher is a survivor in a system that makes it difficult to promote excellence and reward mediocrity. And every parent who gets involved is working against the odds in a system that too often stifles free choice and disregards parental authority.

This last problem holds the key to reforming our schools: *Make the schools once again accountable to the parents and taxpayers of America.*

Under the Clinton Administration, only the unions seem to have a voice. And the reason isn't hard to figure out: One of the most generous supporters to the Clinton-Gore campaign in 1992 was the National Education Association—the most militant of the teachers' unions. In 1992 the NEA chipped in some $600,000 to PACs supporting the Clinton campaign. In the two years before the last congressional election, the NEA gave another $2.3 million to PACs supporting the Democratic Party.

Groups like the NEA command armies of lawyers and lobbyists to fight change. But who speaks for the parents? They don't have political action committees like those who help bankroll the Clinton campaign; they can't afford to cut big checks for candidates who do their bidding.

But they *are* the ones who help pay more than $250 billion every year to support our public schools. We believe they are entitled to have a say in how the schools are run.

COMPETITION AND PARENTAL CHOICE

• *Establish Opportunity Scholarships for students.*

In a Dole Administration, we will establish a four-year, $3 billion demonstration program to provide Opportunity Scholarships worth at least $1,000 for elementary school students and $1,500 for high school students. This initiative will be the largest school choice program ever launched.

That aid will go to those who need it most: to children in

low- and middle-income families who attend any accredited school—public, private, or religious—that chooses to participate. The Dole-Kemp plan will give these parents the same opportunities that upper-income Americans already enjoy.

And because the states and local communities bear prime responsibility for education, those federal funds for the Opportunity Scholarships will be matched each year by $3 billion in state funds. These scholarships will give millions of kids what they need most: Opportunity. And it will give millions of parents what they need most—the power of choice.

No education expert, however well meaning, knows what's in a child's interest better than that child's own mother and father. After all, wealthy citizens have that right of choice. They're not forced to send their kids to schools that aren't doing the job. We believe every family in America should have that right, too.

Give parents the power of choice, and the schools will once again answer to parents. In states around America today, school-choice reforms are making inroads despite the best efforts of the teachers unions and even the federal government.

Milwaukee, Wisconsin, is a good example: In some of the city's school districts, parents receive a voucher from the state. They use that voucher to pay tuition at the school of their choice. The result: rising scores, rising standards, satisfied parents and students, and a healthy dose of competition within the school system.

By returning control of our schools to American parents, we can let them insist and help ensure that no child is forced to attend an unsafe school. With greater parental involvement, local schools can establish the type of disciplinary codes that are essential for a safe and ordered learning environment.

Above all, real competition among schools will push standards higher. Parents will seek out the schools that provide the best curriculum for their children and insist on the highest learning standards.

- *Allow low- and middle-income parents and students to deduct the interest they pay on student loans for post–secondary school education.*

Parents and students who have to bear the high price of higher education often have to carry the added cost of interest on student loans. The Dole-Kemp economic plan wants to make it easier for those who seek higher education as a way of expanding opportunities. This critical change to the tax code will reduce the burden of investing in education.

- *Allow penalty-free withdrawals from an IRA for college education.*

To make it easier for parents to save for their children's education, the Dole-Kemp plan permits penalty-free withdrawals from an IRA that can be used to defray the costs of college tuition, books, or related expenses. This same provision can also be used by adults or their spouses who decide to pursue college education.

- *Allow low- and middle-income parents to establish Education Investment Accounts for their children up to the age of 18.*

The $500 per child tax credit or other funds may be placed into these accounts, up to a limit of $500 per year. For example, parents who invest their $500 per year tax credit in an Education Investment Account will accumulate—at 7 percent interest—over $18,000 by the time their child is ready to enter college.

As with IRAs, accumulated earnings on these accounts will be tax-free if funds are left in the account for at least five years. Money may be withdrawn from these accounts to pay for tuition, fees, books, computers, and other expenses at an accredited college, university, or other post-secondary institution of higher learning.

CREATING A WORLD-CLASS WORK FORCE FOR THE 21ST CENTURY

• *Simplify and strengthen our job-training programs.*

Today there are more than 80 federal job-training, vocational-education, and adult-educational programs. We now spend about $5 billion a year, with no accountability, and studies show these programs are doing very little to help people. The current system is confusing, redundant, ineffective, and expensive.

We have tried job training as a massive and complicated federal effort. And the results are clear: It doesn't work.

In a Dole-Kemp Administration, these will be consolidated into one effective program for helping American workers train for new jobs. That program will take the form of a single grant to the states.

People at the state and local level are far better able to understand the employment needs of workers than are teams of labor experts studying the problem from Washington. Only the states have the flexibility to experiment with new approaches to job training, such as vouchers that workers can use to purchase the training they need from private firms, schools, and community colleges.

• *Allow workers to receive tax-free college, graduate, or post-graduate tuition assistance from employers.*

This means permanently reinstating Section 127 of the Internal Revenue Service Code. Employers should be encouraged to provide tax-free educational benefits to their employees without the involvement of government bureaucracies. These educational benefits will provide more workers with the skills and learning they need to take full advantage of the many new opportunities of today's economy. The change will also allow workers to receive tax-free college, graduate, or post-graduate assistance from employers in order to seek training for a new form of work or in a different field.

• *Increase workers' access to tax-free job search and placement assistance from their employers so they may find another job or prepare for a new trade or business.*

This proposal will expand Section 127 of the Internal Revenue Service Code to encourage employers to provide tax-free outplacement assistance. Under the current rule, employees receive a tax break on such assistance *only* if the assistance is to find a similar job and cash payment is not offered as an alternative to the assistance.

This new rule will play an important role as companies find themselves downsizing, but remaining eager to help assist employees' transition to new occupations. The new rule will allow employers to provide assistance even if (a) the assistance helps prepare the employee for a job in a new trade or business or helps the employee start his or her own business, and/or (b) a cash payment is offered as an alternative to assistance.

PUTTING OUR TRUST IN PEOPLE

Never in human history have children had as many opportunities as our children have today. Never have good schools, and the virtues they instill, been so crucial to our future.

But preparing our children for those opportunities is not the job of distant bureaucrats, complacent unions, or education theorists. It's the job of every parent in America—of free people who take responsibility for themselves, and demand that government reflect their values and trust in their good sense.

CHAPTER 15

COMMON SENSE
IN THE COURTROOM

Like all other institutions in a free society, our courts depend upon people acting responsibly, with self-restraint and a view to the interests of the community. This has not been the case in recent years with America's trial lawyers. Our justice system is in need of serious reform. And that reform must begin with reining in lawyers who are abusing the system for their own selfish ends—at great cost to businesses, to consumers, and to our entire economy.

In a Dole-Kemp Administration, we intend to bring sanity and self-restraint back into a litigation system now out of control.

Everyone understands that consumers need the right of redress in court. At their best, trial lawyers can stand up for citizens and consumers who have been defrauded, misled, or otherwise harmed by an individual or company. Many lawyers still serve that purpose. They are upholding the best traditions of the legal profession. They are doing important and honest work.

But others have stretched the law to its limits. Litigation in modern America has become an industry in itself. Unburdened by any sense of restraint, trial lawyers today seek damages far beyond what reason and fairness allow.

Often they sue for the most innocuous offenses, counting on businesses to strike a settlement just to avoid the exorbitant costs of litigation. The entire system encourages a "go for broke" mentality among trial lawyers, who thrive on the excesses the system allows.

The lawyers' lobby, one of the most powerful in Washington, would like us to think they are champions of the little guy doing battle with corporate greed. More often, it's the other way around.

AMERICA IN THE DOCKET

These abuses of our legal system are a terrible burden on the American economy. When businesses have to pay staggering legal bills, they merely pass the costs on to consumers who buy their products.

In insurance premiums alone, the average American family is paying an extra $200 to cover the costs of phony claims. By one estimate, lawsuit abuse imposes an effective "litigation tax" of $132 billion per year on our economy.

That's money that could have gone to productive uses: Developing new products and technologies; creating jobs and new businesses. But instead of spending that money productively, businesses around America are, in effect, paying a tithe to trail lawyers whose avarice is a drag on our whole economy.

Worse is the whole spirit that this rush to litigation breeds throughout America. Of course the consumer needs access to the courts for reasonable grievances. That right is sacred.

But just as vital to the system is *trust and good will.* Just as basic to civil justice is the self-restraint to act within the bounds of reason and decency. Too often today, trial lawyers are flouting that trust, collecting giant sums for the most minor grievances, and you are paying for it. Our civil courts were not designed to make lawyers into millionaires: They were designed to assure honesty and integrity among all citizens, lawyers included, and to compensate those who have been truly wronged.

We need to bring that integrity back into the system. It can be done with a few simple but bold reforms. Here is what we plan to do.

COMMON SENSE LEGAL REFORMS

- *Limit punitive damages to $250,000 or three times economic damages, whichever is greater.*

This reform will apply to all cases except the most serious—those involving death, serious injury, alcohol or drug use, criminal misconduct, or civil rights violations. It will also apply to all civil cases—not just product liability cases.

In other words, no more outrageous and arbitrary punitive damage awards such as the $2.7 million damages originally awarded to a plaintiff who spilled McDonald's coffee on herself and held the company responsible. Among the many other groups this reform will protect are charitable and volunteer groups, which are often the victims of frivolous and costly lawsuits.

- *Restore the principle of individual responsibility to civil actions.*

This means abolishing the current doctrine of "joint and several liability" for non-economic damages. Under that rule, people only remotely involved in a case may be held fully responsible; you can be only 1 percent responsible but still 100 percent liable. Under our reform, each actor in a lawsuit can be held liable only for his or her fair share of the problem. This will remove the incentive of trial lawyers to drag every possible individual or business into a lawsuit.

- *Promote early settlement of claims to avoid endless and costly lawsuits.*

Under this reform, a defendant could make an "early offer"—within 120 days—to compensate a plaintiff for all economic damages, including medical costs and lost income. The plaintiff may reject the offer and pursue the lawsuit. But in that case, he or she may only recover non-economic damages, including punitive damages, where there is clear and convincing proof the defendant's conduct was caused by intentional or wanton misconduct. States would be able to opt out of this reform.

- *Ensure that the money recovered in settlements goes to those who were injured, not their lawyers.*

We need to place a curb on the contingency fees that now give lawyers an incentive to bring frivolous lawsuits in the hope of winning huge fees. When a defendant offers an acceptable settlement, the plaintiff's lawyer may collect an hourly rate but not a contingency fee.

If, on the other hand, the settlement offer is rejected, the plaintiff's lawyers will only be able to collect a fee to be awarded by a judge or jury that exceeds the original offer. As it is, there are too many incentives for lawyers to abuse our legal system instead of seeking justice. States would be able to opt out of this reform.

CONTROL OUR AUTO INSURANCE BILLS

Why does auto insurance cost so much? Lots of reasons, some of them unavoidable. But one reason is that too many trial lawyers today make their living scavenging our roads and highways in search of clients. Of course there are cases of genuine legal wrong or negligence, but they are far outnumbered by the familiar cases of exorbitant damages sought by lawyers against insurance companies. The companies in turn pass those costs on to customers in the form of higher premiums. One very simple reform could lower our auto insurance bills by hundreds of dollars.

• *Enact a system of "auto choice," allowing car owners to choose their own policies.*

A policy holder could choose a more expensive insurance plan covering economic damages and "pain and suffering," or a cheaper policy covering economic damages only. Any economic damages not covered in the latter policy could be recovered from a negligent driver. Damages for pain and suffering would be available only in cases involving gross negligence or drug and alcohol abuse.

By one estimate, this reform could reduce an average driver's yearly premiums by almost 30 percent—or about $221 per car. States would be able to opt out of this reform. Below is a state-by-state rundown of the savings:

STATE-BY-STATE 1996 SAVINGS FROM AUTO-CHOICE		
Total Savings[1] (Millions)	Estimated 1996 Average Premium	Average Savings Under Auto Choice
All U.S.	$40,037	$773	$221
Alabama	$312	$631	$106
Alaska	$37	$913	$110
Arizona	$777	$878	$306
Arkansas	$337	$691	$193
California	$5,260	$884	$292
Colorado	$672	$891	$273
Connecticut	$987	$924	$362
Delaware	$148	$874	$253
Florida	$2,220	$668	$181
Georgia	$834	$712	$149
Hawaii	$345	$1,081	$439
Idaho	$145	$578	$161
Illinois	$1,393	$679	$164
Indiana	$763	$620	$162
Iowa	$321	$521	$129
Kansas	$87	$638	$45

Kentucky	$61	$700	$25
Louisiana	$1,015	$927	$407
Maine	$180	$538	$168
Maryland	$1,007	$775	$268
Massachusetts	$1,731	$1,093	$430
Michigan	$890	$815	$128
Minnesota	$785	$740	$232
Mississippi	$254	$703	$151
Missouri	$679	$680	$176
Montana	$142	$653	$224
Nebraska	$198	$607	$150
Nevada	$310	$975	$346
New Hampshire	$144	$685	$149
New Jersey	$2,346	$1,093	$395
New Mexico	$272	$870	$288
New York	$3,877	$1,115	$393
North Carolina	$1,088	$554	$170
North Dakota	$17	$507	$31
Ohio	$1,294	$577	$153
Oklahoma	$428	$669	$186
Oregon	$402	$659	$165
Pennsylvania	$1,994	$744	$221
Rhode Island	$156	$1,103	$256
South Carolina	$556	$708	$217
South Dakota	$112	$595	$207
Tennessee	$452	$595	$116
Texas	$2,920	$908	$292
Utah	$217	$708	$196
Vermont	$50	$601	$103
Virginia	$896	$578	$170
Washington	$951	$793	$281
West Virginia	$334	$807	$293
Wisconsin	$704	$569	$176
Wyoming	$52	$609	$147

[1]Assumes 100 percent switch. Based on state laws of 1988.

Sources: Abrahamse and Carroll (1995) and Joint Economic Committee calculations.

Integrity and Responsibility

At every turn these past four years, Bill Clinton has opposed efforts to reform our civil courts. When Republicans and Democrats in Congress joined to curtail frivolous lawsuits, he opposed them. At the urging of the trial lawyers lobby, he vetoed both the securities litigation reform bill and legislation reforming our product-liability system.

This is not our idea of "putting people first" in our courts of justice. It's wrong, pure and simple. The interests of the American people lie in a legal system that prevents abuses by businesses and lawyers alike. The system today is a corruption of what it was meant to be. It rewards the grasping of trial lawyers while often neglecting the truly aggrieved.

We can bring reason and justice back to our civil courts. But it's going to take resolve and character to defy one of Washington's richest lobbies and look instead to the interests of the ordinary citizen.

CHAPTER 16

FREQUENTLY ASKED QUESTIONS:
A Summary of the Dole-Kemp Plan

Will I get a tax cut under the Dole-Kemp Economic Growth Plan?

Yes. All taxpayers get tax relief under our plan. The 15 percent across-the-board tax-rate cut applies to every federal tax bracket.

Who benefits?

The Dole-Kemp plan is designed to provide tax relief to all taxpayers. Tax rates will be cut 15 percent across-the-board. Families with children will receive a $500 per child tax credit. Elderly Americans will benefit from the repeal of Bill Clinton's Social Security benefits tax hike.

How much money will I save on my federal taxes?

How much you will save depends on your income level and family situation. A married couple with two children earning $50,000 per year, for example, will save $1,657 on their federal taxes. That's a savings of nearly 38 percent on their income tax bill. A single taxpayer, with no children, earning $30,000 will save $519, or 15 percent.

Can we cut taxes and balance the budget?

Yes. Government has the responsibility to control spending, and people have a right to keep more of their own earnings. That's why, as we cut taxes across the board, a Dole Administration will lead the effort to pass and ratify a Balanced Budget Amendment to the Constitution. And that's why President Dole will make full use of the line-item veto.

Balancing the budget and freeing our economy are two sides of the same coin: Tax cuts spur economic activity, which expands the tax base. But government has to hold up its end of the bargain by controlling spending. Congress has already approved a plan which would balance the budget by the year 2002. For our plan to work, we only need to restrain federal spending—excluding Social Security, Medicare, and Defense—by an additional 6 percent. That's just six cents on the dollar.

Balancing the budget and cutting taxes are a matter of presidential will. If you have it, you can do it. We have it. We will do it.

Will the tax-cut plan mean cuts in Social Security and Medicare?

No. Social Security is untouched. Medicare spending will actually *increase* from $5,200 per beneficiary to $7,000 per beneficiary by the year 2002 under our plan. That's an increase of $1,800. Anyone who claims our plan hurts Social Security or Medicare is not telling the truth. Since critics have no ideas of their own for getting wages rising and our economy moving, they try to scare the American people away from the tax relief they need and deserve. But the American people will not be fooled.

How can we pay for these tax cuts?

The Dole-Kemp tax cuts are paid in full. We will achieve a balanced budget by year 2002. Our plan starts with the savings already approved by both houses of Congress in June. The additional savings come from three categories: federal spending control, the FCC spectrum auction, and additional savings and reform measures.

Together, these three categories represent $217 billion— about 6 percent of all federal spending excluding Social Security, Medicare, and Defense programs. In other words, six cents on every dollar. A recent "Special Report" by the nonpartisan Tax Foundation called this type of spending restraint "plausible, even minor." The savings in these three categories, plus the savings in Congress's June budget resolution, are enough to both balance the budget and finance the tax reduction.

Will the Dole-Kemp plan help families trying to send their children to college?

Yes—those families are some of the biggest beneficiaries. We will create Education Investment Accounts where parents can invest up to $500 per year to save for a child's college education. A parent who invests $500 per year will accumulate—at, for example, 7 percent interest—over $18,000 by the time their child is ready to enter college. Many families will also be able to deduct interest payments on student loans.

What do the experts say about this tax cut plan?

Our plan has been endorsed by Gary Becker, James Buchanan, and Milton Friedman—all of whom have won a Nobel Prize for their work in economics. It also has the support of Stanford University economist Michael Boskin, who served as Chairman of President Bush's Council of Economic Advisers; Stanford University Professor John Taylor; former

Secretary of State and Secretary of the Treasury George Shultz; Harvard University economist Martin Feldstein, a former chairman of President Reagan's Council of Economic Advisers; and economic policy experts Judy Shelton and John Cogan, among a wide array of others.

Is this a tax cut just for the rich?

No. Our 15 percent tax cut applies across-the-board. It's simple, fair, and treats everyone equally. Middle-income Americans with children have the most to gain because of the child credit. Our goal is to get the economy moving again. A growing economy helps low- and middle-income families; the stagnant economy we have today hurts all low- and middle-income families.

Isn't the economy already doing well?

Under President Clinton, we are seeing the slowest economic expansion in a century. In too many families, both parents have to work to make ends meet. Because taxes are so high, often only one paycheck goes to support the family; the other goes to the government. Wages are stagnant for working Americans. Families are anxious about the future. To those who say our economy is doing well, we respond: America can do better.

What about the taxes I pay when I sell stock from an investment?

The Dole-Kemp plan cuts the capital gains tax rate in half. That means a 50 percent reduction on taxes paid on the profit from selling stock, a farm, or a small business. This provision will produce an explosion of job-creating investment which will help create greater economic opportunity and higher wages.

What about the capital gains taxes I pay when I sell my home?

For most Americans, a home is our biggest investment. Under our plan, Americans who sell a home that has been their primary residence for three of the past five years will not pay capital gains taxes on the first $250,000 of the profit they make from the sale. Americans who have lived in their home for longer than ten years will be eligible for even greater tax exclusions.

I am a retiree. What benefits can I expect from the economic growth plan?

The Dole-Kemp plan provides added benefits to seniors and retirees. In addition to the 15 percent income tax cut, the plan repeals the Social Security tax hike signed by President Clinton in 1993. Seniors living on a fixed income need relief from Bill Clinton's high taxes as much as families and business owners.

What will the tax plan do to simplify the tax system and reform the IRS?

We're not just going to simplify the tax code—we're going to replace it. An across-the-board tax cut is the first step. Fundamental tax reform will follow. In the meantime, we will also allow low- and middle-income Americans with investment income of less than $250 to have all of their taxes withheld. This will free about 40 million taxpayers from the obligation of filing a return at all.

Our plan will also shift the burden of proof in IRS audits from the individual to the federal government. It will put an end to invasive "life-style audits" where there is no evidence of criminal wrongdoing. We want to put the IRS on the side of the taxpayer, not the government.

What will prevent Congress from raising taxes in the future?

The law. We will create a barrier between Washington and your wallet. A Dole Administration will call for a constitutional amendment requiring a 60 percent "Yes" vote in both chambers of Congress before they can raise your income tax rates in the future.

What does the Economic Growth Plan do to promote savings?

The Dole-Kemp Economic Growth Plan helps spur savings by creating additional Individual Retirement Account's (IRAs) for spouses who stay at home. It also creates "American Dream Savings Accounts" and "Education Investment Accounts" that will allow Americans to put aside money tax-free to save for their children's higher-education expenses.

APPENDIX A

"RESTORING THE AMERICAN DREAM"

A speech by Bob Dole introducing his Economic Growth Plan

Chicago, Illinois
August 5, 1996

INTRODUCTION BY GEORGE SHULTZ, FORMER SECRETARY OF THE TREASURY

What a pleasure and honor it is for me to be back in Chicago to introduce Bob Dole and to hear him unveil his plan to lift up the American economy to its full potential.

I first knew Bob Dole going back to my days as Director of the Budget in the Nixon Administration. He was there on the Senate Finance Committee. By the time of the Reagan years, he was chairman of that committee and then our leader in the Senate. (I also served in the Eisenhower Administration, but he's too young to have been around in those days.)

I've argued issues with him, worked problems with him, testified before him, and been grilled by him.

Here are some of the things that I've learned:

- He does his homework and knows what he's talk-ing about—he is a no-nonsense thinker.
- He keeps working at a subject until he's satisfied—he has staying power and follow through.
- He has always been dedicated to balancing the fed-eral budget. He is a real deficit hawk and doesn't fall for gimmicks from people trying to escape the realities.
- He knows that trust is the coin of the realm and you know instinctively when you deal with him that Bob Dole can be trusted.
- He can stand up to a tough decision; no backing down.

The plan he will announce today will balance the budget by the year 2002. You can bank on that. That's the only kind of plan he would put his name on.

But with this plan, America can raise its sights once again to an economy that really sparkles and grows. Bob Dole has had lots of experience with economic policy. He knows that government cannot dictate prosperity. He knows what policies will unleash America so growth and prosperity will happen.

Bob Dole's inauguration next January will be a turning point for this country. On that day, the reins of power will be transferred from those with big ambitions for government, to a leader with big ambitions for the American people.

I have the great pleasure and high honor of introducing to you a great man, a great American.

The next President of the United States, Bob Dole.

REMARKS BY BOB DOLE

It's great to be here. It's great to be able to give this speech before Bill Clinton gets a copy and tries to give it himself.

But let me tell you, this is one speech Bill Clinton will never be able to give.

I am running for president because I believe America can

do better. I believe that every family, wage earner, and small business in America can do better—if only we have the right policies in Washington.

That's why I am here today and that's why I am announcing a program that is the opening salvo in a battle to repeal the current tax code, to end the IRS as we know it, and to get the American family's income moving up again. It is a program to:

- Balance the budget;
- Cut the tax burden on the middle class;
- Provide new educational opportunities for Americans;
- Reform our broken-down lawsuit system;
- End needless federal regulation;
- and restore the promise of the American dream.

It is built on my conviction that we live in a time of unparalleled—and unrealized—promise.

America today is competing in the most dynamic world economy we have ever seen. New markets are opening to American goods and services. Entrepreneurs are developing new technologies and creating products that weren't even imagined a few short years ago.

I believe that America stands on the threshold of a breathtaking future, with greater opportunities for growth and prosperity than at any time in our nation's history.

But we are like an Olympic runner with 50 pound weights attached to our legs. It's time to unshackle the U.S. economy from the big-government ball and chain and "go for the gold."

Our history shows that the greatest force for economic growth, for lifting the poor from poverty, for opening opportunities for productive, fulfilling lives for all, is the force of a free people—free to go where God and their dreams guide them.

That is what built America into the most prosperous, generous nation on earth. And that is what my program is all about.

That is why we are going to balance the budget, cut taxes, and remove the dead weight of government—to unleash the full potential of the American people once again.

Now let me say: the current administration has a different philosophy. Rather than seize the opportunities of this new era, they have taken a "grow slow" approach to economic policy. They had a choice—between a dynamic future that is as great as the aspirations of the American people—or the high-tax, high-spending policies of liberal special-interest politics.

And they chose the special interests over the future of the American people.

My message today is that I will put the American people first.

Let me tell you how I see this administration's economic performance falling short and how I will change it.

Clintonomics has produced an economy that is squeezing the middle class between high-taxes and low-growth. The astounding fact is that we were growing 50 percent faster in 1992, when Bill Clinton described the economy as the worst in 5 decades.

The economy then was roaring out of a recession. It was strong and should have gotten stronger. Instead, this administration has given America the slowest growth of any economic expansion since the last century.

If our economy today could be sent to a doctor, it would be committed to an intensive care ward to be treated for anemia.

In this sputtering economy, some quarters have been better than others. Still, the administration itself projects growth through the end of this decade at an incredibly lackluster 2.3 percent. The Clinton Economic Program has been described as modest—well, it has a lot to be modest about.

Let me say this: In my administration, we won't be satisfied with second, third or fourth best. America will be Number One again.

I believe, that if we are going to compete in the 21st century, we must cut loose from the big-spending special interests and discard the old-style liberal thinking that is holding us back.

We must commit ourselves to a far more ambitious path that puts growth—expanding opportunity, rising incomes, soaring prosperity—at the heart of economic policy.

That is why I want to be president and that is exactly what I will do the day I move into the White House.

I learned long ago, if you don't set ambitious goals, one thing is certain—you'll never reach them.

Bill Clinton's approach to the economy is like the nay-sayers to the space program when John Kennedy said let's go to the moon. He wants to stay earthbound. I say, today, America can reach for the stars.

Let's look at the Clinton record.

The economic insecurity felt by the middle class is not in people's imaginations. You can see it in all the indicators.

The administration rejoiced recently when the unemployment statistics went down. But the reality behind those statistics was nothing to cheer about. The disturbing fact is that we've seen the return of something we thought had disappeared more than a decade ago—the worker who is so discouraged about finding a good job, at a good wage, that he has dropped out of the labor-force and no longer appears in either the employment or unemployment statistics. These are the "Forgotten Workers" of Mr. Clinton's middle-class-squeeze economy.

In my administration the "Forgotten Worker" will be remembered. Growth will put those women and men back on the job, paychecks in their pockets and hope in their hearts once again.

But the "Forgotten Worker" is not the only victim of the Clinton Administration's "squeeze economy." Today millions of Americans are afraid to leave their jobs because they can't find other good opportunities. Economists call it "job lock," and it has been at recession levels since Bill Clinton took office. This means millions of Americans feel trapped, unhappy where they are, not able to realize their potential to the fullest, but with no place else to go.

I give this promise to all Americans who yearn to build a better life: In my administration, we will break the "job lock" and return opportunity to America's working men and women.

During Bill Clinton's presidency, real wages have stagnated and the real median household income has actually dropped. No wonder Americans feel they are working harder and longer and taking home less.

It is as if Bill Clinton has been "downsizing" the entire American economy. I say it's time for us to "upsize" our economy again, and we will, starting on Inauguration Day.

Under Bill Clinton, the personal savings rate has fallen: families aren't able to put away as much for the future, and they've been forced to put more and more on their credit cards just to get by. Meanwhile, productivity growth has been cut in half—causing real raises to be a thing of the past.

The national debt has risen sharply, as have interest rates in the months since Bill Clinton vetoed our balanced budget and twisted arms to defeat the proposed Balanced Budget Amendment to the Constitution. And with that, mortgage rates have risen and the value of homes has virtually stagnated.

This year, Tax Freedom Day—the day when we stop working for the government and start working for ourselves—came later than ever before in American history. The result is that in too many two-income families, one spouse works full-time for the family while the other works full-time for the government.

The fact is, while the administration has waged a class-warfare campaign, the dirty little secret of its middle-class–squeeze economy is that the income of the middle class has fallen, even as the rich have gotten richer.

Think about it: What Clintonomics means is that the rich are getting richer while the middle class gets left behind. We've tried it your way, Mr. President. Now it's time to do something new.

It's time for a new "Independence Day" for the American taxpayer.

Because for too long now, Bill Clinton's liberal policies

have hovered like an alien ship over the American economy, blowing away growth and opportunity.

Well, in 1992—he arrived.

In 1993—he attacked.

In 1996—America strikes back.

And we will bring America back, I promise you that.

Today, as I said, I am announcing my economic program for America's renewal—a program that will return economic growth, rising living standards, and prosperity for all Americans to the center of our policy.

It starts with the "twin necessities" of a balanced budget and tax relief for America's working families.

We have long had a debate in our party about which should come first. Growth advocates say tax cuts first. Fiscal conservatives say a balanced budget first. I say they're both right.

The fact is that the budget deficit and high taxes are two halves of the vise that is producing the Clinton middle-class squeeze.

High taxes pick the American family's pocket directly. Incredibly, that family now spends more on taxes than on food, clothing and shelter combined.

Meanwhile, the budget deficit is a "stealth tax" that pushes up interest rates and costs the typical family $36,000 on an average home mortgage, $1,400 on an ordinary student loan, and $700 on a car loan. Every time a family uses its credit card, it pays a "stealth tax" to the federal government.

There is no magic in fixing this problem. With today's pro-growth Republican Congress, cutting taxes and balancing the budget are just a matter of presidential will. If you have it, you can do it. I have it. I will do it.

I will support and work for the Balanced Budget Amendment.

I will reduce the size of the federal government.

I will balance the budget by the year 2002.

As I am doing that, I will follow the example of many Republican governors across this country. I will reduce taxes while I am balancing the budget.

My program follows two principles: no dollar should be

taxed that would go to providing the basics for a family and no dollar should be taxed that would go to creating a job.

In my administration, the "squeeze economy" will be replaced with an opportunity economy.

The press has done a good job in getting the word out about this program. They say it's "dramatic." It *is* dramatic. Let me tell you about it.

To put it in a nutshell: I intend to lower the federal income tax bill of a family of four making $35,000 a year by 56 percent—cutting it by more than half.

Let me repeat that: This tax reduction will mean that such a middle-class family will take one dollar out of every two dollars that they now pay in income tax and put it right back in their own pockets.

And more dollars will also stay with the women and men who own the smaller businesses that will create the jobs those families depend on.

We will do this by:

First, a 15 percent across-the-board tax cut that will repeal the Clinton tax hike on the middle class. In fact, it will return total taxes to where they were when Ronald Reagan left office.

Second, we will give every middle-income family a $500 per child tax credit. That's a tax credit, not a deduction. That means, if you're raising one child, take back $500. If you're raising two children, take back $1,000. Three children, $1,500, and so on. Those are dollars from your paycheck that should go to your family and that I am determined *will* go to your family.

Third, we will cut the top rate of the capital gains tax in half—because the capital gains tax hits smaller and growing businesses hardest, and they're the ones who will create most of our new jobs in the decade ahead. I want those businesses to use their growing value to give people better jobs, better opportunities, and better incomes—not just to pay more taxes.

Fourth, I will call for expansion of Individual Retirement Accounts so that people can put more away for their old age;

and I will call for a repeal of the 1993 Clinton tax hike on Social Security benefits.

Finally, I will call for a supermajority—a 60 percent vote of Congress—before income tax rates can ever be raised again on the American people.

Let me be absolutely clear: I don't want to be president because I like how things are going now. I *don't* like how things are going. I want to make America better and I know that we *can* make America better, for everyone. And this program is the first step.

As of this moment, Bill Clinton and his party are the defenders of the status quo. We are the party of change.

And this is only the beginning—Phase One.

We will not stop until we repeal the entire tax code and replace it with a simpler, fairer, flatter system that will allow Americans to file their tax returns without the help of a lawyer or an accountant, or both.

Let me give you one example—an important example—of what this first phase will mean. Today, in too many families both spouses work because they have to work. When we have achieved our goal, if both spouses work, it will be because they want to work, not because one is forced to by higher taxes.

Our objective is to spur growth to a healthy, vibrant 3.5 percent a year or more. The naysayers will say that's too ambitious—but the truth is they're not ambitious enough. In the last 5 expansions, the American economy averaged 4.4 percent growth. The post–World War II average—counting recessions—was 3.3 percent. We were growing, as I mentioned, at 3.7 percent before Clinton's big-government policies put the breaks on our economy. The question is: Why is the Clinton Administration selling our economy and the American people short? Why have they given up on the American dream?

We're going to give the engine of the American economy a full tune-up and a new tax filter—to filter out big-government residue—and get it humming again the way it ought to be.

History has shown us that tax cuts, by stimulating growth, bring in more revenue. But let me be clear—the purpose of tax cuts is to leave more money where it belongs—in the hands of the working men and women who earned it.

Of course, as this is an election year, Bill Clinton has promised again that he will cut taxes—not raise them—if you give him another chance in the next four years. But when he tells you that, ask yourself this question: How many times has he kept his word in the last four years?

My program does not stop with low taxes and a balanced budget. One of the costs of stuffing a size-ten government in our size-eight pocketbooks is that the IRS has taken an ever bigger, more oppressive role in American life—and this in itself has become a drag on growth.

Today the IRS is twice as big as the CIA and five times as big as the FBI. It takes the equivalent of nearly three million people working full time—more people than serve in the U.S. Armed Forces—just to comply with our tax laws.

The other day I met a woman in Tennessee. She told me about her two-year fight with the IRS. It's cost her time, heartache, and now they're threatening to seize her property. And what's got the IRS so angry?—a dispute over $127. Gotta hand it to those guys, they really know how to spend the taxpayers' money.

We're going to downsize the IRS and upsize the amount of money Americans get to keep.

I'm an optimist. I believe the IRS can be retrained to do something useful.

I'll start by shifting the burden of proof in IRS audits so that taxpayers in America are once again presumed innocent until proven otherwise.

I will end the IRS's KGB-like "life-style audits" where there is no clear evidence of criminal activity. I will eliminate IRS-filing for 40 million low- and middle-income taxpayers, privatize many IRS functions, modernize the rest, and shift the duties of IRS personnel so that their job is to help Americans give the right answers on their forms, not to punish them for innocent mistakes.

In short, my administration will free the American people from tax tyranny. I will eliminate the IRS as we know it.

In my administration the Clinton regulatory assault on economic growth will also end.

- We will thoroughly review all new and existing regulations to determine what works, what doesn't, what's too expensive, and what's too oppressive.
- And we will end the Clinton exemption to the IRS on the Paperwork Reduction Act.
- I will insist that what the American people get from regulations is more than what they pay to comply with them.

Lawsuit reform is also part of my program. A few months ago, I met a little girl whose life depends on a medical device that may not be available in a few years because of the litigation explosion that has corrupted our civil justice process. Our out-of-control lawsuit system is a drag on growth and undermines competitiveness—driving up prices for all Americans, and even endangering the lives of some, while making a few predatory trial lawyers fabulously wealthy. Even Democratic Senator Jay Rockefeller accused President Clinton of—quote—"selling out to special interests and raw political considerations" when he vetoed our lawsuit reform bill at the behest of the trial lawyers—Clinton's biggest campaign contributors.

In a Dole Administration, we will reform our broken-down lawsuit system. We will:

- Put a limit on outrageous punitive damage awards;
- Revoke the trial lawyers' license to search for deep pockets;
- Curb the abuse of the contingency fee system to ensure that most of the award money goes to those who were injured, not lawyers;
- Change auto insurance laws so that car owners have more choice as to the kind of coverage they buy;

- Promote early settlement of claims by reducing the incentives lawyers have to run up fees by keeping lawsuits alive instead of settling.

In my administration, the predatory, ambulance-chasing trial lawyers will no longer have a special friend in the White House—the American people will.

Finally, economic reform requires getting children and workers ready for the jobs of the future. The Clinton Administration puts our educational future in the hands of bureaucrats and the liberal ideologues of the national teachers' unions. I will do things differently. My program includes:

- "Opportunity Scholarships for Children" that will enable parents to chose the best school for their child.
- Allowing low- and middle-income students and parents to deduct interest on student loans; and giving them the opportunity to set up tax-free "Education Investment Accounts" with the $500 from their annual per child tax credit.
- Allowing workers to receive tax free education grants from their employers.
- And increasing workers' access to tax-free job placement assistance from their employers.

In short, I will take education out of the hands of the unions and bureaucrats and put it back in the hands of parents—where it belongs.

Now, I know there are going to be a lot of questions about this economic program from our friends in the press—particularly about the tax cuts I have proposed. Fine. Let's have a debate on economic growth, and let's start with a few of the questions that will surely be asked:

Question Number One: Aren't you abandoning your commitment to cutting the deficit?

Let me tell you something, I grew up a poor boy in Russell, Kansas. I know the importance of living within your means and

I know the consequences of not doing that. Deficit reduction is in my blood and a balanced budget will be my legacy to America.

President Clinton will tell you a balanced budget is impossible—at the same time he has vetoed two balanced budgets, proposed one of the biggest pork-barrel spending programs in American history, passed the biggest tax hike in history, and submitted a budget of his own which forecast deficits as far as the eye could see. What is impossible for a Democratic president captured by liberal, special-interest spending pressures, is eminently doable for a Republican president with a Republican Congress—especially when the president is armed with the line-item veto.

I will be that president. I will get it done.

Question Number Two: Aren't you just proposing a tax cut for the rich?

No, I'm going to give tax relief to every single taxpayer in America.

I know the Democrats will revert to their same old mantra, "Tax breaks for the rich, tax breaks for the rich." Of course, their definition of rich is anyone who has a job.

There is one constant in American life: a growing economy is good for the middle class; a stagnant economy is bad. I will restore vitality and growth to the American economy.

Question Number Three: Isn't this program a return to the—quote—"failed" policies of the eighties?

Let's talk about the 1980s: During the Reagan years, we vanquished inflation, brought interest rates down from double digits and averaged nearly four percent economic growth in the longest, peacetime expansion in history.

I take great pride in my reputation as a deficit hawk. But let me also say one of my proudest achievements was helping to pass Ronald Reagan's historic, across-the-board tax cut. That tax cut helped restore America's economic greatness.

I want to return to tax cuts—this time balancing the budget with a Republican Congress and finishing the job Ronald Reagan started so brilliantly but could not complete because the Democrats refused as usual to reduce spending.

Just as we rolled back the Soviet Empire in the 1980s, we're going to roll back the empire of liberal, big-spending special interests and big government in the latter half of the 1990s.

Finally, people will ask **Question Number Four:** Bill Clinton's spin doctors have their own numbers showing that everything is great. Their motto is, "Don't Worry, Be Happy." Who are we to believe?

Let me suggest this simple test: Ask yourself, do you believe America is on the right track today? And do you believe that we are building a future that is better for our children?

When I finish here today, a lot of commentators will try to tell you who this program is for. So before they do, let me tell you who in my mind it is for.

I'm thinking of the mother who works, just as her husband works, because one income is no longer enough to make ends meet.

The mortgage payment on their house just went up, because interest rates jumped between one-and-a-quarter and two percent after Bill Clinton vetoed our balanced budget package, and she's wondering where she'll find the extra money.

She works in a small company, the kind that has created most of America's new jobs over the last decade and a half— except that it hasn't been growing since Bill Clinton passed his tax increase on the "rich." The owner can't afford to invest in its growth, and as a result, the pay raises that used to come regularly have stopped coming.

Her husband works for a big company. But even as it has found itself in a new, more competitive global market, it has been hit by one new regulation after another at home. There's been talk of corporate downsizing, and she's not sure what the next year will bring.

As Americans always have, she wants her children to have a better life. But the schools seem worse than when she was growing up and they can't afford a private school. She wonders if her kids will be ready for the world they graduate into.

The family's taxes have crept up over the years until today they're paying tax rates that only millionaires used to pay.

She knows that, if taxes were down and growth was up to the level of the mid-eighties, the family could make ends meet.

This mother and her family are the ones my program is for.

They are the reason I want to cut taxes and regulations and balance the budget; end the litigation explosion and revitalize education and training.

You might ask if I know such a family and the answer is, yes, I do. Many things have changed since I was a boy, but the story is the same now as it was then. The families described could be my family, my next door neighbors, or the people down the street—the farmer's family and the shopkeeper's family and the teacher's family in my hometown. We all worked. We all struggled to make ends meet. We all knew what it meant to struggle in Russell, Kansas.

So who am I doing this for? I'm doing it for mothers, and fathers, and children—for families all over America.

That's why I am running for president.

So that as we enter the new century, America will be stronger, freer, more vibrant and hopeful than ever before; more nurturing of its families, with greater opportunities for each and every American to pursue his or her dreams.

As Winston Churchill said so many years ago, "Give us the tools and we will finish the job." I say today that if we give America a new birth of freedom, there is no limit to what the American people can achieve.

I know in my heart, our best days are yet to come.

Thank you and God bless you.

APPENDIX B

"A BETTER AMERICA"

A speech by Bob Dole

Republican National Convention
San Diego, California
August 15, 1996

Ladies and gentlemen, delegates to the convention, and fellow citizens, I cannot say it more clearly than in plain speaking. I accept your nomination to lead our party once again to the Presidency of the United States.

And I am profoundly moved by your confidence and trust, and I look forward to leading America into the next century. But this is not my moment, it is yours. It is yours, Elizabeth. It is yours, Robin. It is yours, Jack and Joanne Kemp.

And do not think I have forgotten whose moment this is above all. It is for the people of America that I stand here tonight, and by their generous leave. And as my voice echoes across darkness and desert, as it is heard over car radios on coastal roads, and as it travels above farmland and suburb, deep into the heart of cities that, from space, look tonight like strings of sparkling diamonds, I can tell you that I know whose moment this is: It is yours. It is yours entirely.

And who am I that stands before you tonight?

I was born in Russell, Kansas, a small town in the middle of the prairie surrounded by wheat and oil wells. As my neighbors and friends from Russell, who tonight sit in front of this hall, know well, Russell, though not the West, looks out upon the West.

And like most small towns on the plains, it is a place where no one grows up without an intimate knowledge of distance.

And the first thing you learn on the prairie is the relative size of a man compared to the lay of the land. And under the immense sky where I was born and raised, a man is very small, and if he thinks otherwise, he is wrong.

I come from good people, very good people, and I'm proud of it. My father's name was Doran and my mother's name was Bina. I loved them and there's no moment when my memory of them and my love for them does not over-shadow anything I do—even this, even here—and there is no height to which I have risen that is high enough to allow me to forget them—to allow me to forget where I came from, and where I stand and how I stand—with my feet on the ground, just a man at the mercy of God.

And this perspective has been strengthened and solidified by a certain wisdom that I owe not to any achievement of my own, but to the gracious compensations of age.

Now I know that in some quarters I may not—may be expected to run from this, the truth of this, but I was born in 1923, and facts are better than dreams and good presidents and good candidates don't run from the truth.

I do not need the presidency to make or refresh my soul. That false hope I will gladly leave to others. For greatness lies not in what office you hold, but on how honest you are in how you face adversity and in your willingness to stand fast in hard places.

Age has its advantages.

Let me be the bridge to an America than only the unknowing call myth. Let me be the bridge to a time of tranquility, faith and confidence in action.

And to those who say it was never so, that America's not been better, I say you're wrong. And I know because I was there. And I have seen it. And I remember.

And our nation, though wounded and scathed, has outlasted revolutions, civil war, world war, racial oppression and economic catastrophe. We have fought and prevailed on almost every continent. And in almost every sea.

We have even lost. But we have lasted, and we have always come through.

And what enabled us to accomplish this has little to do with the values of the present. After decades of assault upon what made America great, upon supposedly obsolete values, what have we reaped? What have we created? What do we have?

What we have in the opinions of millions of Americans is crime and drugs, illegitimacy, abortion, the abdication of duty, and the abandonment of children.

And after the virtual devastation of the American family, the rock upon which this country was founded, we are told that it takes a village, that is collective, and thus the state, to raise a child.

The state is now more involved than it ever has been in the raising of children. And children are now more neglected, more abused, and more mistreated than they have been in our time.

This is not a coincidence. And with all due respect, I am here to tell you it does not take a village to raise a child. It takes a family to raise a child.

If I could by magic restore to every child who lacks a father or a mother that father or that mother, I would. And though I cannot, I would never turn my back on them. And I shall as President vote measures that keep families whole.

And I'm here to tell you that permissive and destructive behavior must be opposed. That honor and liberty must be restored and that individual accountability must replace collective excuse.

And I'm here to say to America, do not abandon the great traditions that stretch to the dawn of our history. Do not topple the pillars of those beliefs—God, family, honor, duty, country—that have brought us through time, and time again.

And to those who believe that I am too combative, I say

if I am combative, it is for love of country. It is to uphold a standard that I was born and bred to defend. And to those who believe that I live and breathe compromise, I say that in politics honorable compromise is no sin. It is what protects us from absolutism and intolerance.

But one must never compromise in regard to God and family and honor and duty and country. And I'm here to set a marker, that all may know that it is possible to rise in politics, with these things firmly in mind, not compromised and never abandoned.

For the old values endure and though they may sleep and though they may falter, they endure. I know this is true. And to anyone who believes that restraint honor and trust in the people cannot be returned to government, I say follow me.

Only right conduct distinguishes a great nation from one that cannot rise above itself. It has never been otherwise.

Right conduct every day, at every level, in all facets of life. The decision of a child not to use drugs; of a student not to cheat; of a young woman or a young man to serve when called; of a screenwriter to refuse to add to mountains of trash; of a businessman not to bribe; of a politician to cast a vote or take action that will put his office or his chances of victory at risk, but which is right.

And why have so many of us—and I do not exclude myself, for I am not the model of perfection—why have so many of us been failing these tests for so long? The answer is not a mystery. It is to the contrary quite simple and can be given quite simply.

It is because for too long we have had a leadership that has been unwilling to risk the truth, to speak without calculation, to sacrifice itself.

An administration, in its very existence, communicates this day by day until it flows down like rain and the rain becomes a river and the river becomes a flood.

Which is more important, wealth or honor?

It is not as was said by the victors four years ago, the

economy, stupid. It's a kind of nation we are. It's whether we still possess the wit and determination to deal with many questions including economic questions, but certainly not limited to them. All things do not flow from wealth or poverty. I know this firsthand and so do you.

All things flow from doing what is right.

The cry of this nation lies not in its material wealth but in courage, and sacrifice and honor. We tend to forget when leaders forget. And we tend to remember it when they remember it.

The high office of the presidency requires not a continuous four-year campaign for re-election, but rather broad oversight and attention to three essential areas: the material, the moral, and the nation's survival in that ascending order of importance.

In the last presidential election, you the people were gravely insulted. You were told that the material was not only the most important of these three, but in fact, really the only one that mattered.

I don't hold to that for a moment. No one can deny the importance of material well-being. And in this regard, it is time to recognize we have surrendered too much of our economic liberty. I do not appreciate the value of economic liberty nearly as much for what it has done in keeping us fed, as to what it's done in keeping us free.

The freedom of the marketplace is not merely the best guarantor of our prosperity. It is the chief guarantor of our rights, and a government that seizes control of the economy for the good of the people ends up seizing control of the people for the good of the economy.

And our opponents portray the right to enjoy the fruits of one's own time and labor as a kind selfishness against which they must fight for the good of the nation. But they are deeply mistaken, for when they gather to themselves the authority to take the earnings and direct the activities of the people, they are fighting not for our sake but for the power to tell us what to do.

And you now work from the first of January to May just

to pay your taxes so that the party of government can satisfy its priorities with the sweat of your brow because they think that what you would do with your own money would be morally and practically less admirable than what they would do with it.

And that simply has got to stop. It's got to stop in America.

It is demeaning to the nation that within the Clinton Administration, a core of the elite who never grew up, never did anything real, never sacrificed, never suffered and never learned, should have the power to fund with your earnings their dubious and self-serving schemes.

Somewhere, a grandmother couldn't afford to call her granddaughter, or a child went without a book, or a family couldn't afford that first home because there was just not enough money to make the call, or to buy the book, or to pay the mortgage. Or, for that matter, to do many other things that one has the right and often the obligation to do.

Why? Because some genius in the Clinton Administration took the money to fund yet another theory, yet another program and yet another bureaucracy. Are they taking care of you, or are they taking care of themselves?

I have asked myself that question. And I say, let the people be free. Free to keep. Let the people be free to keep as much of what they earn as the government can strain with all its might not to take, not the other way around.

I trust the American people to work in the best interest of the people. And I believe that every family, wage earner and small business in America can do better—if only we have the right policies in Washington, D.C.

And make no mistake about it, my economic program is the right policy for America and for the future, and for the next century.

Here's what it will mean to you. It means you will have a president who will urge Congress to pass and send to the states for ratification a Balanced Budget Amendment to the Constitution.

It means you will have a president and a Congress who have the will to balance the budget by the year 2002. It means you will have a president who will reduce taxes 15 percent across-the-board for every taxpayer in America.

And it will include a $500 per child tax credit for lower- and middle-income families in America. Taxes for a family of four making $35,000 a year would be reduced by more than half—56 percent to be exact. And that's a big, big reduction.

It means you will have a president who will help small businesses, the businesses that create most new jobs, by reducing the capital gains tax rate by 50 percent. Cut it in half. It means you will have a president who will end the IRS as we know it.

It means you will have a president who will expand individual retirement accounts, repeal President Clinton's Social Security tax increase, provide estate tax relief, reduce government regulations, reform our civil justice system, provide educational opportunity scholarships and a host of other proposals that will create more opportunity for all Americans and all across America.

And I will not stop there. Working with Jack Kemp and a Republican Congress I will not be satisfied until we have reformed our entire tax code and made it fairer and flatter and simpler for the American people.

The principle involved here is time-honored and true, and that is, it's your money. You shouldn't have to apologize for wanting to keep what you earn. To the contrary, the government should apologize for taking too much of it.

The Clinton Administration just doesn't get it. And that's why they have got to go.

The president's content with the way things are. I am not. We must commit ourselves to a far more ambitious path that puts growth, expanding opportunities, rising incomes and soaring prosperity at the heart of national policy.

We must also commit ourselves to a trade policy that does not suppress pay and threaten American jobs. And by any measure, the trade policies of the Clinton Administration has been a disaster. Trade deficits are skyrocketing and middle-income families are paying the price.

My administration will fully enforce our trade laws and not let our national sovereignty be infringed by the World Trade Organization or any other international body.

Jack Kemp and I will restore the promise of America and get the economy moving again, and we'll do so without leaving anybody behind.

And I have learned in my own life, from my own experience that not every man, woman or child can make it on their own. And that in time of need, the bridge between failure and success can be the government itself. And given all that I have experienced, I shall always remember those in need. That is why I helped to save Social Security in 1983 and that is why I will be the president who preserves and strengthens and protects Medicare for America's senior citizens.

For I will never forget the man who rode on a train from Kansas to Michigan to see his son who was thought to be dying in an Army hospital. When he arrived, his feet were swollen and he could hardly walk because he had to make the trip from Kansas to Michigan standing up most of the way.

Who was that man? He was my father. My father was poor and I love my father. Do you imagine for one minute that as I sign the bills that will set the economy free, I will not be faithful to Americans in need? You can be certain that I will.

For to do otherwise would be to betray those whom I love and honor most. And I will betray nothing.

Let me speak about immigration. Yes. Let me speak about immigration. The right and obligation of a sovereign nation to control its borders is beyond debate. We should not have here a single illegal immigrant.

But the question of immigration is broader than that, and let me be specific. A family from Mexico arriving this morning legally has as much right to the American Dream as the direct descents of the Founding Fathers.

The Republican Party is broad and inclusive. It represents many streams of opinion and many points of view.

But if there's anyone who has mistakenly attached themselves to our party in the belief that we are not open to citizens of every race and religion, then let me remind you, tonight this hall belongs to the Party of Lincoln. And the exits which are clearly marked are for you to walk out of as I stand this ground without compromise.

And though I can only look up, and at a very steep angle, to Washington and Lincoln, let me remind you of their concern for the sometimes delicate unity of the people.

The notion that we are and should be one people rather than "peoples" of the United States seems so self-evident and obvious that it's hard for me to imagine that I must defend it. When I was growing up in Russell, Kansas, it was clear to me that my pride and my home were in America, not in any faction, and not in any division.

In this I was heeding, even as I do unto this day, Washington's eloquent rejection of factionalism. I was honoring, even as I do unto this day, Lincoln's word, his life and his sacrifice. The principle of unity has been with us in all our successes.

The 10th Mountain Division, in which I served in Italy, and the Black troops of the 92nd Division who fought nearby were the proof for me once again of the truth I'm here trying to convey.

The war was fought just a generation after America's greatest and most intense period of immigration. And yet when the blood of the sons of immigrants and the grandsons of slaves fell on foreign fields, it was American blood. In it you could not read the ethnic particulars of the soldier who died next to you. He was an American.

And when I think how we learned this lesson I wonder how we could have unlearned it. Is the principle of unity, so hard-fought and at the cost of so many lives, having been contested again and again in our history, and at such a terrible price, to be casually abandoned to the urge to divide?

The answer is *no*.

Must we give in to the senseless drive to break apart that which is beautiful and whole and good?

And so tonight I call on every American to rise above all that may divide us, and to defend the unity of the nation for the honor of generations past, and the sake of those to come.

The Constitution of the United States mandates equal protection under the law. This is not code language for racism. It is plain speaking against it.

And the guiding light in my administration will be that in this country, we have no rank order by birth, no claim to favoritism by race, no expectation of judgment other than it be even-handed. And we cannot guarantee the outcome, but we shall guarantee the opportunity in America.

I will speak plainly on another subject of importance. We're not educating all of our children. Too many are being forced to absorb the fads of the moment.

Not for the nothing are we the biggest education spenders and among the lowest education achievers among the leading industrial nations.

The teachers' unions nominated Bill Clinton in 1992. They're funding his re-election now. And they, his most reliable supporters, know he will maintain the status quo.

And I say this—I say this not to the teachers, but to their unions. I say this, if education were a war, you would be losing it. If it were a business, you would be driving it into bankruptcy. If it were a patient, it would be dying.

And to the teachers' union, I say, when I am president, I will disregard your political power for the sake of the parents, the children, the schools and the nation. I plan to enrich your vocabulary with those words you fear—school choice and competition and opportunity scholarships.

All this for low- and middle-income families so that you will join the rest of us in accountability, while others compete with you for the commendable privilege of giving our children a real education.

There is no reason why those who live on any street in America should not have the same right as the person who lives at 1600 Pennsylvania Avenue—the right to send your child to the school of your choice.

And if we want to reduce crime and drug use and teen pregnancies, let's start by giving all our children a first-class education.

And I also want these children to inherit a country that is far safer than it is at present. I seek for our children and grandchildren a world more open and with more opportunity than ever before.

But in wanting these young Americans to be able to make the best of this, I want first and foremost for them to be safe. I want to remove the shadow that darkens opportunities for every man, woman and child in America.

We are a nation paralyzed by crime. And it's time to end that in America.

And to do so, I mean to attack the root cause of crime—criminals, violent criminals.

And as our many and voracious criminals go to bed tonight, at say, 6:00 in the morning, they had better pray that I lose this election because if I win, the lives of violent criminals are going to be hell.

During the Reagan Administration, we abolished parole at the federal level. In the Dole Administration we will work with the nation's governors to abolish parole for violent criminals all across America. And with my national instant check initiative, we will keep all guns out of the hands of criminals.

And I have been asked if I have a litmus tests for judges. I do.

My litmus test for judges is that they be intolerant of outrage; that their passion is not to amend, but to interpret the Constitution that they are restrained in regard to those who live within the law, and strict with those who break it.

And for those who say that I should not make President Clinton's liberal judicial appointments an issue in this campaign, I have a simple response. I have heard your argument.

The motion is denied.

I save my respect for the Constitution, not for those who would ignore it, violate it, or replace it with conceptions of their own fancy.

My administration will zealously protect civil and constitutional rights while never forgetting that our primary duty is protecting law abiding citizens, everybody in this hall.

I have no intention of ignoring violent—I said violent criminals, understanding them, or buying them off. A nation that cannot defend itself from outrage does not deserve to survive. And a president who cannot lead itself against those who prey upon it does not deserve to be President of the United States of America.

I am prepared to risk more political capital in defense of domestic tranquility than any president you have ever known. The time for such risk is long overdue.

And in defending our nation from external threats, the requirements of survival cannot merely be finessed. There is no room for margin of error. On this subject perhaps more than any other, a president must level with the people and be prepared to take political risks. And I would rather do what is called for in this regard and be unappreciated, than fail to do so and win universal acclaim.

And it must be said because of misguided priorities there have been massive cuts in funding for our national security. I believe President Clinton has failed to adequately provide for our defense. And for whatever reason the neglect, it is irresponsible.

I ask that you consider these crystal-clear differences. He believes that it is acceptable to ask our military forces to do more with less. I do not.

He defends giving a green light to a terrorist state, Iran, to expand its influence in Europe. And he relies on the United Nations to punish Libyan terrorists who murdered American citizens. I will not. He believes that defending our people and our territory from missile attack is unnecessary. I do not.

And on my first day in office, I will put America on a course that will end our vulnerability to missile attack and rebuild our armed forces.

It is a course President Clinton has refused to take. And

on my first day in office, I will put terrorists on notice. If you harm one American, you harm all Americans. And America will pursue you to the ends of the earth.

In short, don't mess with us if you're not prepared to suffer the consequences.

And furthermore, the lesson has always been clear, if we are prepared to defend, if we are prepared to fight many wars and greater wars than any wars that come, we will have to fight fewer wars and lesser wars and perhaps no wars at all.

It has always been so and will ever be so. And I'm not the first to say that the long gray line has never failed us, and it never has.

For those who might be sharply taken aback and thinking of Vietnam, think again. For in Vietnam the long gray line did not fail us, we failed it in Vietnam.

The American soldier was not made for the casual and arrogant treatment that he suffered there, where he was committed without clear purpose or resolve, bound by rules that prevented victory, and kept waiting in the valley of the shadow of death for 10 years while the nation debated the undebatable question of his honor.

No, the American soldier was not to be thrown into battle without a clear purpose or resolve, not made to be abandoned in the field of battle, not made to give his life for indifference or lack of respect. And I will never commit the American soldier to an ordeal without the prospect of victory.

And when I am president every man, and every woman in our armed forces will know the president is Commander-in-Chief, not Boutros Boutros-Ghali or any other UN Secretary General.

This I owe not only to the living, but to the dead, to every patriot, to every patriot grave, to the ghosts of Valley Forge, of Flanders Field, of Bataan, the Chosin Reservoir, Khe Sanh, and the Gulf.

This I owe to the men who died on the streets of Mogadishu not three years ago, to the shadows on the bluffs of Normandy, to the foot soldiers who never came home, to the airmen who fell to earth, and the sailors who rest perpetually at sea.

This is not an issue of politics, but far graver than that. Like the bond of trust between parent and child, it is the lifeblood of the nation. It commands not only sacrifice but a grace in leadership embodying both caution and daring at the same time. And this we owe not only to ourselves. Our Allies demand consistency and resolve, which they deserve from us as we deserve it from them. But even if they falter, we cannot, for history has made us the leader, and we are obliged by history to keep the highest standard possible.

And in this regard may I remind you of the nation's debt to Presidents Nixon, Ford, Reagan, and Bush. President Nixon engaged China and the Soviet Union with diplomatic genius. President Ford, who gave me my start in 1976, stood fast in a time of great difficulty, and with the greatest of dignity. Were it not for President Reagan, the Soviet Union would still be standing today.

He brought the Cold War to an end, not, as some demanded, through compromise and surrender—but by winning it. That's how he brought the Cold War to an end.

And President Bush, with a mastery that words fail to convey, guided the Gulf War coalition and its military forces to victory. A war that might have lasted years and taken the lives of tens of thousands of Americans passed so swiftly and passed so smoothly that history has yet to catch its breath and give him the credit he is due.

History is like that. Whenever we forget its singular presence, it gives us a lesson in grace and awe.

And when I look back on my life, I see less and less of myself and more and more a history of this civilization that we have made that is called America.

And I am content and always will be content to see my own story subsumed in great events, the greatest of which is the simple onward procession of the American people. What a high privilege it is to be at the center in these times—and this I owe to you, the American people.

I owe everything to you. And to make things right, and to close the circle, I will return to you as much as I possibly can. It is incumbent upon me to do so. It is my duty and my deepest desire. And so tonight, I respectfully ask for your blessing and your support.

The election will not be decided by the polls or by the opinion-makers or by the pundits.

It will be decided by you.

And I ask for your vote so that I may bring you an administration that is able, honest, and trusts in you.

For the fundamental issue is not of policy, but of trust—not merely whether the people trust the president, but whether the president and his party trust the people, trust in their goodness and their genius for recovery.

That's what the election is all about.

For the government cannot direct the people, the people must direct the government.

This is not the outlook of my opponent—and he is my opponent, not my enemy.

And though he has tried of late to be a good Republican . . . and I expect him here tonight . . . there are certain distinctions that even he cannot blur. There are distinctions between the two great parties that will be debated and must be debated in the next 82 days.

He and his party brought us the biggest tax increase in the history of America. And we are the party of lower taxes and greater opportunity.

We are the party whose resolve did not flag as the Cold War dragged on. We did not tremble before a Soviet giant that was just about to fall, and we did not have to be begged to take up arms against Saddam Hussein.

We are not the party, as drug use has soared and doubled among the young, hears no evil, sees no evil, and just cannot say, "Just say no."

We are the party that trusts in the people. I trust in the people. That is the heart of all I have tried to say tonight.

My friends, a presidential campaign is more than a contest of candidates, more than a clash of opposing philosophies.

It is a mirror held up to America. It is a measurement of who we are, where we come from, and where we are going. For as much inspiration as we may draw from a glorious past, we recognize American preeminently as a country of tomorrow. For we were placed here for a purpose, by a higher power. There's no doubt about it.

Every soldier in uniform, every school child who recites the Pledge of Allegiance, every citizen who places her hand on her heart when the flag goes by, recognizes and responds to our American destiny.

Optimism is in our blood. I know this as few others can. There once was a time when I doubted the future. But I have learned as many of you have learned that obstacles can be overcome.

And I have unlimited confidence in the wisdom of our people and the future of our country.

Tonight, I stand before you tested by adversity, made sensitive by hardship, a fighter by principle, and the most optimistic man in America.

My life is proof that America is a land without limits. And with my feet on the ground and my heart filled with hope, I put my faith in you and in the God who loves us all. For I am convinced that America's best days are yet to come.

May God bless you. And may God bless America. Thank you very much.

APPENDIX C

"A WORLD OF HOPE"

A speech by Jack Kemp

Republican National Convention
San Diego, California
August 15, 1996

Abraham Lincoln believed you serve your party best by serving our country first. Ladies and gentlemen, I cannot think of a better way of serving our nation than by electing Bob Dole President of the United States of America.

And by the way, this time let's reelect a Republican Congress to help Bob Dole restore the American dream. That's what is important in 1996. It's just that we need to re-elect our Republican Congress.

Tonight, here in San Diego, Bob Dole and I begin this campaign to take our message of growth, hope, leadership, and cultural renewal to all Americans.

As I said in Russell, Kansas, Bob Dole's hometown, last Saturday, we're going to take our cause from the boroughs of New York to the barrios of California. We're not going to leave anyone out of this cause and this campaign.

We're going to carry the word to every man, woman and child of every color and background that today, on the eve of the new American century, it's time to renew the American promise and to recapture the American dream, and to give our nation a new birth of freedom with liberty, equality and justice for all. That's what it means to be a Republican.

Tonight, I'm putting our opponents on notice. We're going to ask for the support of every single American. Our appeal of boundless opportunity crosses every barrier of geography, race and belief in America. We're not going to leave anybody out of this opportunity

We may not get every vote. Now, listen to me for a moment. We may not get every vote, but we'll speak to every heart. In word and action, we will represent the entire American family. That's what we must be all about.

And so, in the spirit of Mr. Lincoln, who believed that the purpose of a great party was not to defeat the other party. The purpose of a truly great party is to provide superior ideas, principled leadership and a compelling cause, and in that spirit, I accept your nomination for the Vice Presidency of the United States of America.

Thank you. OK, I accept, I accept, I accept. I had to say it.

Our convention is not just the meeting of a political party; our convention is a celebration of ideas. Our goal is not just to win, but to be worthy of winning.

This is a great nation with a great mission, and last night we nominated a leader whose stature is equal to that calling, a man whose words convey a quiet strength, who knows what it means to sacrifice for others, to sacrifice for his country, and to demonstrate courage under fire; who brings together all parties and backgrounds in a common cause.

In recent years it has been a presidential practice when delivering the State of the Union address to introduce heroes in the balcony. Next year, when Bob Dole delivers the State of the Union address there'll be a hero at the podium.

There is another hero with us tonight. He's here in our hearts, he's here in our spirit. He's here in our minds. He brought America back and restored America's spirit. He gave us a decade of prosperity and expanding horizons. Make no mistake about it, communism came down, not because it fell, but because he pushed it.

Thank you, Ronald Reagan. The Gipper.

Our campaign—for just a moment, let me talk about this campaign, this cause—is dedicated to completing that revolution. I'm sure he's watching us. So let me just say to him, on behalf of all of us who love him, thanks to the Gipper.

And tonight is the party of Abraham Lincoln and Ronald Reagan and Bob Dole, and all the great Republicans who precede us and upon whose shoulders we stand, we begin our campaign to restore the adventure of the American dream.

With the end of the Cold War, all the "isms" of the 20th century—Fascism, Nazism, Communism, Socialism, and the evil of Apartheidism—have failed, except one. Only democracy has shown itself true to the hopes of all mankind. We must be that party

You see, democratic capitalism is not just the hope of wealth, but it's the hope of justice. When we look into the face of poverty, we see the pain, the despair and need of human beings. But above all, in every face of every child, we must see the image of God.

You see, the Creator of All has planted the seed of creativity in every single one of us, the desire within every child of God to work and build and improve our lot in life, and that of our families and those we love. And in our work, and in the act of creating that is part of all labor, we discover that part within ourselves that is divine. I believe the ultimate imperative for growth and opportunity is to advance human dignity.

Dr. Martin Luther King believed that we must see a sleeping hero in every soul. I believe America must establish policies that summon those heroes and call forth their boundless potential and that of the human spirit. But our fullest potential will never be achieved by following leaders who call us to timid tasks, diminished dreams and some era of limits.

You see, every generation faces a choice: hope or

despair—to plan for scarcity or to embrace the possibilities. Societies throughout history believed they had reached the frontiers of human accomplishment. But in every age, those who trusted that divine spark of imagination discovered that vastly greater horizons still lay ahead.

You see, Americans do not accept limits. We transcended those limits. We do not settle for things as they are. We are intent on succeeding.

I learned this as a lesson as a young boy growing up in the street in Los Angeles, California. My dad was a truck driver.

My daddy was a truck driver. He and my uncle bought the truck, started a trucking company, put four boys through college. From them and my mom, a teacher, I learned to never give up. Now I want you to know tonight, from the bottom of my heart, to me, faith, freedom, and family, as well as life, are the greatest gifts of God to all humanity. It is precious and we need to be that party.

Today America is on the threshold of the greatest period of economic activity, technological development, and entrepreneurial adventure in the history of the world. We have before us tomorrows that are even more thrilling than our most glorious of yesterdays.

And yet the genius of the American people is being stifled. Our economy is growing at the slowest pace in any recovery in this century. The income of working men and women in America is dropping or stagnant. And there's kind of a gnawing feeling throughout our nation that—in some way, for some reason—just something wrong.

Our friends in the other party say the economy is great. It's moving forward. It's moving, like a ship dragging an anchor, the anchor of taxes, and excessive regulations and big government and bureaucracy.

They say it's the best we do and the best we can hope for. But that's because they have put their entire trust in government rather than people. They want a government that runs our lives, runs our businesses, runs our schools. You see, they just don't believe in the unlimited possibilities that freedom can bring.

Today, the Democratic Party is not democratic. They are elitist. They don't have faith in people. They have in government. They trust government more than markets. And that's why they raised taxes on middle-income families. That's why they tried to nationalize health care. That's why that today they say they are "unalterably opposed" to cutting taxes on the American family.

That's the problem with elitists—they think they know better than the people. But the truth is, there's a wisdom, there's an intelligence in ordinary women and men far superior to the greatest so-called experts that have every lived. That's what our party must be all about.

The Democratic Party is the party of the status quo. And as of tonight, with Bob Dole as our leader, we are the party of change.

Our first step will be to balance the budget with a strategy that combines economy in government with the type of tax cuts designed to liberate the productive genius of the American people.

Now, of course, the naysayers in the Clinton White House say it can't be done. They've got to say that. They don't know Bob Dole and they don't know Jack Kemp.

As Bob and I have said before and will continue to say throughout this campaign, with a pro-growth Republican Congress, balancing the budget while cutting taxes is just a matter of presidential will. If you have it, you can do it. Bob Dole has it. And Bob Dole will do it.

You can count on it.

And guess what?

All the critics aside, I'm going to be with him, at his side, every step of the way. And so will you.

But this is just the beginning. This is the first step.

We're going to scrap the whole fatally flawed tax code of America, and replace it with a flatter, fairer, simpler, pro-family, pro-growth tax code for the 21st century. We can do it.

And guess what? Guess what? That's rhetorical. You don't have to answer.

We're going to end the IRS and its intrusiveness as we have known it these past 83 years.

We're going to start with a 15 percent across-the-board tax rate cut. There's going to be tax relief and a $500 per child tax credit. We're going to cut the capital gains tax in half, and not apologize for it.

We're going to take the side of the worker, the side of the saver, the entrepreneur, the family. The American people can use their money more wisely than can government. It's time they had more of a chance, and we're going to give them that opportunity, that chance.

That's what this is all about.

Here we are, on the eve of the 21st century, in the middle of that technological revolution that is transforming the world in which we live. But how can it be that so many families find themselves struggling just to keep even, or just to get by?

And I want to say this from the heart—that as long as it takes two earners to do what one earner used to do, how can anybody say this economy is good enough for the American people?

Our tax cut will mean that parents will have more time to spend with their children—and with each other. It means that a working parent can afford to take a job that lets them maybe be home when the kids come home from school. It means that the struggling, single mother in the inner city of America will find it easier to get out of poverty and to work off the welfare system which is a drag on her hopes and aspirations.

We cannot forget, my friends, that a single mom and her children in this country cannot be left out of our great revolution for this country.

The American society as a whole can never achieve the outer-reaches of its potential so long as it tolerates the inner cities of despair. And I can tell you that Bob Dole and Jack Kemp will not tolerate that despair in our nation's cities.

I read the account by a reporter when I was at Housing and Urban Development, I read the account of a reporter of his conversation with a 10-year-old child at Henry Horner public housing in Chicago, which I had had the honor of visiting.

The reporter told in his book that he asked the little boy what he wanted to be when he grew up. The little boy said, "If I grow up, I'd like to be a bus driver."

He said, "If I grow up." He said "If"—not when. At the age of 10 he wasn't sure he'd even make it to adulthood.

Think how much poorer our nation is, and deprived of, not allowing that child to reach his or her potential. And those like him. Think how much richer our nation will be when every single child is able to grow up to reach for his or her God-given potential—including those who come to America. Including those who are willing to risk everything to come to this nation.

My friends, we are a nation of immigrants. And as the former president of Notre Dame University, Father Theodore Hesburgh, said, the reason we have to close the back door of illegal immigration is so that we can keep open the front door of legal immigration.

That is what it means to be in America.

You see, our goal is not just a more prosperous America, but a better America. An America that recognizes the infinite worthwhile of every individual and, like the Good Shepherd, leaves the 99 to find the one stray lamb.

An America that honors all its institutions—the values that moms and dads want to pass on to their children.

An America that makes the ideal of equality a daily reality— equality of opportunity, equality in human dignity, equality before the laws of mankind as well as in the eyes of God.

An America that transcends the boundaries between the races with the revolutionary power of the simple, yet profound idea to love our neighbors as ourselves.

We must remember all that is at stake in America's cultural renewal—not just the wealth of our nation but the meaning as well.

Today, more than ever before, America's ideals and ideas grip the imaginations of women and men in every corner of the globe. And isn't it exciting—isn't it exciting to think, that it's 1776—only this time all over the world?

You know, President Reagan spoke of America as a shining city on a hill, a light unto nations. And in decades past, so many of those who looked for that light did so from behind a wall and barbed wire, and tyrannical regimes.

Now, because the American people stood strong, those people are free.

Freedom is not free. It's never guaranteed. Our nation and its president must be strong enough to stand up for freedom against all who would challenge it.

A world of peace. A world of hope. That's what America's economic and cultural renewal means at home and around the world. This is what our cause is all about. This is why we'll elect Bob Dole the next president. This is why we need a Republican Congress.

And I want you to know, the other night I was honored, I was so honored to be part of that tribute, so meaningfully to President Reagan. Afterwards. Mrs. Reagan said she was touched by my calling Ronald Reagan the last lion of the 20th century. Well, I said history will record that.

I believe America is fortunate that last night you, and you, and you nominated a leader worthy of succeeding President Reagan—a man with the strength, the determination and the vision to do the job that lies ahead.

And I want you to know tonight from the bottom of my heart, I believe Bob Dole will be the first lion of the 21st century.

Thank you.

APPENDIX D

WHY THE DOLE-KEMP PLAN WILL WORK

Gary S. Becker,
1992 Winner of the Nobel Prize in Economics

I was surprised when I received a phone call in early May to attend a meeting in Washington with then–Senate Majority Leader Bob Dole of Kansas, other senators, and a few economists to discuss the formulation of an economic program for the Presidential campaign. I had been the consummate Washington outsider: I declined all invitations to testify before Congress and had never even set foot in the Capitol, the building where the meeting was to take place!

But I accepted this invitation because I believed that new economic initiatives were much needed to raise the growth rate of America. The meetings with Dole and his advisers gave me a priceless education on the mix of economic and other factors that determine an economic program.

It was agreed early on that cuts in income and capital gains taxes were to be the centerpiece of his program. I believed large cuts were essential; their precise form mattered much less. Dole choose a 15 percent across-the-board tax cut from several alternatives because families can easily understand how that would directly affect them. Moreover, this cut is a major step toward the reforms he promised for his first presidential term: a simpler and flatter tax structure, a Balanced Budget Amendment to the Constitution, and the requirement of super-majorities in Congress to raise income-tax rates.

From the beginning, Dole wanted major education and training initiatives because he recognizes that investments in human capital are essential to robust long-term growth in modern economies that depend on knowledge, skills and information. Better education and training will also help narrow the inequality in earnings that has grown over the past two decades.

Vouchers and Savings. His program advocates scholarships, or vouchers, for students from middle-class and poor families, that could be spent at private schools, including parochial schools. Poorer students attend the worst public schools, since they cannot afford either private schools or good suburban schools. Vouchers, choice, and competition among schools, sharply distinguish Dole's approach from President Clinton's, since he, along with the teachers' unions, has strongly opposed school vouchers and choice.

The Dole plan includes education savings accounts that allow families to contribute $500 per year to an "education individual retirement account" for each child, which can be spent eventually on college or other post–high school education. It also gives tax incentives to companies to pay for training and retraining of employees—including those who lost their jobs possibly because of downsizing.

The Dole program plans to first stop and then roll back the rapid growth in regulations under Presidents George Bush and Bill Clinton. The Clinton Administration itself estimates that the cost of complying with federal regulations in 1995 absorbed almost 10 percent of gross domestic product, and the cost is continuing to rise. Dole would require benefit-cost analysis to justify new regulations and would reevaluate all existing regulations.

Feedback. I believe the full program can reach the target of 3.5 percent growth per year. The U.S. and many other countries have enormous reservoirs of skills that are throttled by high taxes, excessive regulation, and failures to properly educate and train much of the work force. Any country will gain a large burst in economic vitality if it can improve opportunities for men and women to start businesses and encourage much greater investments in human and physical capital.

The tax cuts and other incentives in the Dole program would reduce federal revenues by about $550 billion over the six-year period to the year 2002. Faster economic growth and reallocation of assets toward more taxable forms induced by the whole program, not just the tax cuts, is assumed to recover during this six-year period about 27 percent, or $150 billion, of the revenue loss.

I consider this 27 percent feedback conservative. Martin S. Feldstein of Harvard University has estimated that the 1996 tax cuts yield a 40 percent feedback. More than $200 billion, rather than the assumed $150 billion, will be recovered in six years if the Dole package raises growth by only 0.2 percentage points each year for six years: Instead of growing at 2.2 percent each year, the economy would grow at 2.4 percent in the first year, 2.6 percent in the second, and so on.

Some critics label the assumption of revenue recovery voodoo economics revisited, but to me it is a simple application of elementary economics taught to freshmen: that powerful changes in incentives have powerful effects on behavior. Economists should go out of business if they deny that taxes, prices, and costs significantly alter behavior. This is the strength of Dole's economic plan.

APPENDIX E

JUST THE FACTS ON DOLE'S ECONOMIC GROWTH PLAN

Michael J. Boskin, Former Chair,

President's Council of Economic Advisers
August 25, 1996

Bob Dole's comprehensive economic growth program—which features tax cuts and reform, enough savings to balance the budget and education, job training, regulatory and legal reforms—has been met by ferocious and disingenuous attacks, orchestrated by White House spinmeisters and their allies.

"Voodoo II! You cannot cut taxes and balance the budget—that's incredible! It will cost $800 billion!" These are but some of the hyperbolic charges levied by White House political hacks and economic advisers.

What's really in the Dole program to raise family incomes and create greater opportunity? The program would slow the growth of spending, leading to declining deficits and a balanced budget by 2002. A 15 percent across-the-board reduction in tax rates and a $500 per child credit would bring tax relief to 90 million American families. The capital gains tax rate would be cut to a maximum of 14 percent, unlocking trillions of dollars in capital to create new jobs and businesses.

Individual Retirement Accounts would be expanded to increase savings. President Clinton's 1993 tax increase on Social Security recipients would be repealed. And a super-majority (60 percent) vote would be required in Congress to raise income tax rates. As a downpayment on fundamental reform to a flatter, fairer, simpler tax system to be implemented in the next several years, the Internal Revenue Service would be made more taxpayer friendly.

There are a number of additional proposals that have not been as widely reported. These include education and job training reform focused on choice and competition; allowing deductibility of interest on student loans; tax-exempt Education Investment Accounts; tax-exempt college tuition assistance from employers; increasing workers' access to tax-free job search and placement assistance from employers; and consolidating more than 100 job training programs into a single grant to the states, which would be encouraged to experiment with innovative private-sector approaches.

Cost benefit analyses would be required for new major federal regulations. The government would have to review and reevaluate regulations every four years and enforce the Paperwork Reduction Act (which Clinton has ignored). Legal reforms include limits on punitive damage awards; promotion of early settlement of claims; curbs on abusive contingency fee representation; auto choice reforms that could dramatically lower insurance premiums; and reforming the joint and several liability doctrine, which encourages lawyers to sue everyone in sight for the entire amount of damages, even if they had only a tangential relationship to the alleged illegal activity.

A married couple with two children earning $30,000 per year would get a 71 percent reduction in their federal income tax; a couple earning $50,000 would have a 38 percent reduction; a couple earning $100,000 would see their federal income tax reduced by 24 percent.

The overall "cost" as estimated by Dole's own economic team (including myself) is $548 billion. White House economic adviser Gene Sperling, whose reputation for making up numbers is documented in recent books on the 1992 campaign, says it will cost more than $800 billion. The non-partisan Joint Committee on Taxation of Congress, the official scorekeeper, confirms the Dole team's estimates.

How is it paid for?

Here is where the voodoo economics straw man comes into play. "Dole is claiming the tax cuts will pay for themselves." The same argument was hurled ferociously at President Reagan in 1981 and has been used to try to discredit Reagan's policies ever since. The charge is simply fallacious. First, the Dole program assumes that a modest 27 percent of the revenue would be recouped by some combination of higher incomes and less tax sheltering.

The historical evidence from the 1980s tax cuts, and the symmetric evidence from the 1990s tax increases, suggest that the figure is more likely 40 percent to 50 percent. Thus, the Dole assumptions are conservative.

Second, Reagan never said his tax cuts would pay for themselves. The Reagan team also assumed a modest revenue reflow. What happened in the 1980s was that the tax share in the economy was stabilized, not reduced, by tax cuts and indexing of tax brackets. The revenue reflows from the rate cuts were substantial, but not sufficient overall to pay for themselves. The culprit for the deficits in the 1980s was that spending went up, not down, because Congress would not control it.

The savings in the Dole plan, not only to finance the tax cut but to balance the budget by the year 2002, come from slower growth in overall spending, including some outright cuts. About two-thirds of these were expressly laid out in the Dole program—the $393 billion in the 1996 Congressional Joint Budget Resolution.

Of the remaining approximately $200 billion needed to get to a balanced budget, Dole has laid out a variety of potential options. A 10 percent across-the-board reduction in the administrative expenses of government would save $90 billion for example.

The charges that the Dole plan is vague are thus simply ludicrous. This is far and away the most specific any presidential contender has been in history. Compare it with

Clinton's 1992 Putting People First plan, almost all of which was just hyperbolic rhetoric. When costed out, Clinton's program would have produced a revenue shortfall of between half a trillion and a trillion dollars. That is one of several reasons he pushed the largest tax increase in history rather than his middle-class tax cut.

No one suggests that the spending constraint will be easy, but surely it will be within the grasp of a President Dole, receiving budgets from a Republican Congress, able for the first time to use a line-item veto to reject even Republican pork.

The Dole plan makes sense. The numbers are credible, despite the barrage of criticisms from the White House and its allies. Consider the source: The president's 1993 economic plan claimed $500 billion in deficit reduction, conveniently ignoring all of the increased spending that reduced this total to a little more than $300 billion. They also claimed they had the same amount of spending cuts as tax increases, by redefining what was spending and what was taxes; the real ratio was five dollars of tax increases to every dollar of spending cuts. The same group told us that the president's health care plan—a monster in its own right—had numbers that were "bulletproof" or "airtight." When serious economists, including myself, examined these numbers, they were short by $100 billion a year, and even their own party leaders termed them "fantasy."

As Sgt. Joe Friday on the old television series *Dragnet* used to say, "Just the facts." Well, those are the facts, folks. Make up your own mind.

INDEX